MAN CAVE UNDER CONSTRUCTION

COUNTING THE COST

Stephen B. Wright

WESTBOW
PRESS®
A DIVISION OF THOMAS NELSON
& ZONDERVAN

This book is a work of non-fiction. Unless otherwise noted, the author
and the publisher make no explicit guarantees as to the accuracy of
the information contained in this book and in some cases, names
of people and places have been altered to protect their privacy.

WestBow Press books may be ordered through booksellers or by contacting:

WestBow Press
A Division of Thomas Nelson & Zondervan
1663 Liberty Drive
Bloomington, IN 47403
www.westbowpress.com
844-714-3454

ISBN: 978-1-9736-7371-2 (sc)
ISBN: 978-1-9736-7378-1 (hc)
ISBN: 978-1-9736-7372-9 (e)

Library of Congress Control Number: 2019913125

Print information available on the last page.

WestBow Press rev. date: 09/22/2022

CONTENTS

DEDICATION

I dedicate this book to the memory and ministry of my father, the late Rev. H. D. Wright. A family man and role model who provided wisdom, advice, and life lessons.

To my mother, Dolly Nelson Wright, whose instructions toward life were instrumental in my development.

To my son, Steven B. Wright, who is learning what manhood entails.

To my best friend and wife, Paulette, who pushed me to complete this book.

NOWHERE TO SOMEWHERE

Sometimes as a man, I feel like getting into my car at night and driving it to nowhere, drawing a square, then unfolding my chair, sitting in the dark, as I intently stare ...into nowhere. Expressing how life is so unfair, how many burdens I may bare, sighing ungratefully as I breathe God's graced air.

God simply says, "Cast me your cares, go down in prayer, you are an heir." So I erase the square, fold up my chair, and drive back to somewhere, fully aware that God is everywhere.

—Stephen B. Wright

INTRODUCTION

I am an ordained and licensed minister who has learned that the more you study the Bible, the more there is to be learned. There is a need to do an exegesis of a biblical text to discover the context and intended meaning of the writers. Who was the writer? Who was the audience? What was the intent of the message? Similarly, the more you learn about yourself, the more you need to learn why you are who you are. The infrastructure of human existence is entangled with lies and truth, pain, hurt, love and hate; however, we are expected to excavate and recover that which is required to sustain a normal and healthy life. At times, what was communicated to us and what we interpreted were two different things. As I set out to write this book, I wanted to focus on man's human blueprint to identify with some of our common complexities, such as health, and influences that lead to our demise, however, it is critical to evaluate the foundational essence of man, which is spiritual. This brings into question: do we know what we think we know? *Man Cave Under Construction* examines this.

The man cave, in this book, is not a physical place where you extract yourself from the realities of a busy life, watch sports, or do absolutely nothing, but rather a vantage point to which we have learned to see life. In this, we seek to construct beyond what or how we understand, in hopes of allowing ourselves to expand. It isn't the reality, but the idea of manhood that creates in every man a pattern of predictable behaviors. This book originally covered three aspects of manhood—the man, husband, and father—in response to the question: why do we think the way we do? However, I decided to revise this book to focus on the first aspect alone. *The Other Side of You* and *The Extension of You* will be explored in separate books. This book is intended to be an amalgamation between the spiritual and natural man so that man's reality in Christ may be revealed.

Purpose of the book

This book is designed to help men build a life that mirrors their spiritual walk. We must not assume that once you are born again everything falls into place or you know everything. We must be positioned to be successful both spiritually and in our humanity through prayer and teaching. 1 Timothy 2:4 (KJV) states, "Who will have all men to be saved, and to come unto the knowledge of the truth." "To come" is from the Greek word erchomia, meaning to come from one place to another. It is a progressive growth in the knowledge of Christ. This should be the quest after salvation. Likewise, we grow in our human acquisitions, so too we can also explore the truth about our influences, and traditions in families and communities.

We can't afford to let past brokenness, failures, and carnality become the blueprint imprinted in our minds and be the foundation for which we build. The impressions that are with us have influenced our actions, and unless our influences change, our actions will remain the same. As men of God, the spirit of God should influence our minds, and our minds influence our actions. This book also attempts to bring clarity to our understanding, focusing on what we have been taught through scripture and human interaction. The constructs that form the totality of what we believe about manhood may be subject to reconstruction, especially if it was constructed with misinformation. Even though intentions were good, the information was based on what was familiar to those who taught us based on how they understood in their time. We should keep those that benefit us while relinquishing those things of which we now have a better understanding.

I don't consider this book a biblical interpretation of manhood, but in some areas, I seek to give context where verses from the bible are used. In many cases, I use biblical metaphors, rhetorical questions, etc. to complement observations of relevant human experience. After all, the experiences of biblical characters were shaped by their customs and manners, but some practical messages contained within are still useful, as we understand our realities in Christ. The first five books of Moses were the building blocks of the Psalms and Prophets, which Jesus points out were about Him. Some of their actions were symbolic and could not fulfill what would be fulfilled through Christ. From a natural perspective, we operate based on the norms and structures of the society around us. This activity governs our human existence. From a spiritual perspective, the most important factor in our lives is the salvation granted by Jesus's death, burial, and resurrection. This is the gospel. The message of the Bible is salvation. This relates to our eternal existence; however, we can't vacate our responsibility in human existence.

Intended Image

> Genesis 1:26 (KJV) "Let us make man in our image and after our likeness"

What is the blueprint or identity of man? The original man was to be designed in the image and likeness of God, possessing God's nature, the full composite of God. What we see here in this verse is God's intent. We will see this is only possible through the redemptive work of Christ in the regenerated man due to Adam's eventual sin. The first question to be asked of this is then what is the image of God, and secondly, are we created in it? John 4:24 (KJV): "God is spirit..." Therefore, the nature of God is spirit. However, let's revisit and take another look to excavate a truth. The original man was created, but all men since have been the product of procreation. We are made in the likeness of the DNA of our parents. You are the imprint or carbon copy of your parents in appearance and genetics. Everyone since Adam produces after its kind. Since the fall of Adam, every man was reproduced in a state of separation from God. Consequently, because of this, we bore the identity of that fallen state.

The first man created originally was without sin, yet all the rest of us either were or are in sin based on acceptance of Christ. Through observation, we are excluded from being "The image of God" based on context. It is therefore impossible to claim to be in the image of God without salvation, which requires hearing and receiving the Gospel of Christ: His death, burial, and resurrection according to the scriptures. Let me explain. In Colossians 1:15 (NLT), it is said, "Christ is the visible image of the invisible God." It is through accepting Christ that we take on this image. Romans 8:29 (KJV): "For whom he did foreknow, he also did predestinate to be conformed to the *image of his Son*, that he might be the firstborn among many brethren." The pretext in Romans 8:15 (KJV): "...or ye have not received the spirit of bondage again to fear; but ye have received the Spirit of adoption, whereby we cry, Abba, Father." We become sons by way of adoption through the redemptive work of Christ. It is through this that we take on the image of our Father. He then becomes the "source" of our existence because His Spirit is in us. We are not the Genesis 1:26 image of God, but rather the Romans 8:29 image of His Son. 2 Corinthians 5:17 (KJV) "Therefore, if anyone *is* in Christ, *he is* a new creation." The image of God in us with the spirit of God being the proof via us believing the message of the finished work of Christ. The new creation is the result of the Resurrection of Christ.

Influenced Image

When we are born into this world, we take on the mental framework of those by whom we are influenced—not only as it relates to sin, but in our everyday realities. We take on the DNA of our parents and are subject to their influence. We take on their identity through genetics, (appearance and physical traits including health), their name through birth, which consists of standards and reputation which devise its own set of rules which you may be required to upkeep. For example, you may be expected to go to the military because it is a requirement for making men in every generation. Any deviation could be a dishonor to the name or leave a stigma. The influence may be a distinct structure within the confines of human traditions while others have no boundaries and are free to operate independently of any Rite of Passage as a classification for manhood.

In addition, we are a template or a transferred imprint of someone's frame of thought. We build from a Framework based on our exposures. This becomes the image that we project. We often follow those who make an impression on us. This may be outside influences unrelated to family. At times, we imitate their actions, build from their blueprint, or quote their words. We sometimes take what they speak as truth, and this can translate into a conviction that is difficult to turn away from. Even when their words are not true, we can commit to their misconstruction by subscribing to their propaganda. Here is something to consider, with influences, you must be careful of bits and pieces of truth that lead to an untruth. All you have is proportional sound bites that sound true until the full dialogue is revealed. This could be intentional or unintentional. Unclear of whether it is good, bad, or indifferent, most of our decisions are derived from the people who influence us, and we are only as good as the information we possess. The problem is that in some cases, context is not carried over. When you are subject to the influence, you must also understand the conditions surrounding the why or the state of mind, because this could have pertained only to the situation at hand, without necessarily having universal application. Like that of a biblical student of detail, you must sit where they sat, hear what they heard, and understand it only in the context in which it was spoken.

For example, when Paul said in Philippians 4:13 (KJV), "I could do all things through Christ," this did not refer to all things as we may think about it or relate them to. The detail in the pretext provides clarity – "It was about contentment or making do in whatever situation he found himself in." (v10-12) But you would have to know these preceding details to understand this. So, if you are an apprentice of someone's instruction or influence, be conscious enough to ask about the context. Without context, we can become either a product of bad teaching or a product of bad understanding. Either way, it can influence the thoughts that produce your actions. Details are required so that a person being influenced understands what is being communicated or what situation to apply it to.

For instance, Genesis 3 (KJV) illustrates the aftermath of the demise that man brought upon himself. It deals with the activities of the physical man after the Fall. These activities were not the result of an act of God, but rather an absence of Him. Often, we attribute things to God that are associated with the acts of man or the influence of the devil, like that of Genesis 2. Revelation 20:2 (KJV) refers to the Devil as "the old Serpent" which refers to the *influencer* in Genesis 3:1(KJV). In the Old Testament God took most of the blame for evil activities simply because of their limited knowledge of an evil entity. The one behind the activities was the least mentioned character. He was the metaphoric "throw a rock and hide your hand" personality of the Old Testament. It is this misleading information that creates and normalizes an inaccurate pattern of thinking of God's personality.

A good example is 1 Samuel 16:14 (KJV): "But the Spirit of the LORD departed from Saul, and an evil spirit from the LORD troubled him." Let us view this in light of the epistles, which are often used to explain the Old Testament. The Old Testament is often referenced as the "Scriptures" in New Testament writings (John 5:39, Luke 24;25-27;44-47, 1 Corinthians 15:14). 1 John 1:5 (KJV) says, "This then is the message which we have heard of *him*, and declare unto you, that *God is light*, and in him is *no darkness at all*." Darkness here refers to evil or sin. We see this through v.6. So, if there is no evil in God, then no evil can come from God. Also, see Psalm 92:15. Samuel experienced something evil, and since God was the only character in the equation, he concluded in assumption what he could not explain. As a result, he attributed this event to God; however, evil can't proceed from Good. For example, if I worked in an office with three people, and something came up missing, I would assume it had to be the other three in the office, not realizing that someone could have come in from the outside.

This demonstrates the primary point in 1 Samuel, which is that an evil spirit cannot come from God but rather is present when God is absent. Such instances, whether spiritual or physical, must be reviewed with understanding, especially if they become foundational for a belief. Fundamentally, an examination or explanation of scripture must be undertaken to gain a clear understanding, otherwise whenever anything at all happens, good or bad, we will, like Samuel, attribute it to God. Events such as pandemics or other catastrophes are good examples of the kinds of things, I have in mind here. Today, Insurance companies and others use the term "Act of God" for that which they can't explain. In 1 Samuel, when the Spirit departed, it simply referred to a separation or absence from God, and when God is absent, evil is then present. In this, you can't say that God did what is not in his nature to do. The real enemy should be attributed to a lack of understanding. Destruction in every facet is the work of evil influences and men doing evil deeds, which cannot be acts of God but the result of his absence.

The foundation of hope should be built on the light of Christ, who said, "The Son can do nothing of himself, but what he seeth the Father do: for what things soever he doeth, these also doeth the Son likewise (John 5:19(KJV). This further communicates the nature of God demonstrated through the incarnate son who said "For the Son of Man did not come to destroy men's lives but to save them" Luke 9:56 (KJV). Jesus implicates the source of destruction in John 10:10a "The thief cometh not, but for to steal, and to kill, and to destroy." The thief here is implied as one with evil intent or from an evil source, so as believers we are obligated to deconstruct our perception of God by disseminating the sources of both good and evil. This is a prime example of how an unaudited view, idea, or concept can shift the landscape of thinking for a lifetime.

There is a clear demarcation, that is the Blueprint or DNA between God and Satan. The Blueprint of God is life and life and light. The enemy's DNA is to kill, steal, and destroy. It would be a miscarriage of justice for God to take the wrap for the enemy's work when it does not match His DNA or blueprint. Besides, He has already paid the price to deliver us from the enemy's hold via salvation. Since it is God's "will all men be saved", (1 Timothy 1:4 KJV) it suggests that the only one who benefits from man's untimely death pre-salvation is the enemy.

Neither the time of death nor death itself is God's doing. 1 Corinthians 15:26 (NIV) indicates death is "the last enemy to be destroyed." God does not partner with his enemy. If a man was told to stop smoking by his physician or he would die but he continues who is responsible for his untimely death? If a man is a part of a gang who engages in a gang shoot-out daily and dies, who is responsible for his untimely death? He is because it was his choice to ignore those things that led to his demise. Let us validate this argument with scripture. Let's take a close look at Ephesians 6:1-3(KJV) which is quoted from Exodus 20:12. "Children, obey your parents in the Lord, for this is right. "Honor your father and mother," which is the first commandment with promise: "that it may be well with you and you may live long on the earth." It implies that untimely death could be the result of our choices and activities.

Expressions of our image

Since this book parallels our humanity, the way you are communicated to others is the way others will see you, unless that perception is otherwise clarified.

The identity of a man is found in what he communicates. What he communicates is discovered in what he believes, and what he believe is a sum of influences, experiences, and expectations. People show you what they want you to see by discrediting what you don't see. These influences lead to conscious and deliberate bias that plays out in our conscious and subconscious thinking. For instance, if you are shown several videos of a certain demographic of people in a negative light, it influences your perception of them. So, when you go out in public, you associate a similar group with what you saw, although they are not. As a result, you may treat them with a negative response. In essence, we communicate through filters of how we see the world or rather how we allow it to be introduced to us. This seems to suggest that communication is a constructed idea, a reflection of our thoughts. Communication in this context consists of verbal and nonverbal communication, which includes actions.

How we communicate, whether we know it or not, is based on these things we adhere to and is filtered by both our subconscious and our conscious thoughts. These things produce within us a conviction with which we communicate and, in turn, which we develop a bias or a reception to certain things communicated. Most often, our filters allow us to engage according to their relevance. In other words, if it does not agree with how we see things, we filter it out. This relevance is the way we connect over common beliefs, experiences, or expectations. Information contrary to your filters may lead to rejection or conflict within the communication. This is primarily because within those three filters, to name just a few, are your ideas, dreams, opinions, and adversely, possibly your fears, pain, hurt, hatred, and bitterness. Subsequently, these filters will determine whether we accept or reject what is heard. This supports the idea that we are the products of our constructive thoughts.

The convictions of our filters can be so strong that we miss context and jump to conclusions that were never introduced. At times, what we hear are words or terms that remind us of past instances that are reintroduced into the present moment. I call these trigger words because they can draw us into emotional experiences even during an unemotional event. This suggests that we implicate people in the present based on what someone else did in the past. If not them, what they are communicating. We must listen with the intent to gain an understanding of what is being communicated to us within the context of the conversation. This means that your experiences or expectations should not elicit a response based on your filters. This implies that you should probably ask questions to gain clarity if required. Not everyone has been exposed to what we have been exposed to and vice versa. They too have filters that are likely to be different from yours. The quest for communication means we sometimes must allow unlikely people inside of our filtration systems, with the intent to learn and to see from the other side.

Sometimes, the challenge for men is filtering out in the same manner that we filter in. We filter information based on beliefs, experiences, and expectations; however, we may filter out through walls. This means that others are not allowed to see us as openly as we see them. This is sometimes the mode of operation of man. In our attempt to not communicate our insecurities, we default to the idea that "some things are better left unsaid." This leads to shallow relationships or depending on the type of relationship, it could even be interpreted as neglect. Details are the voice of reasoning to misunderstandings. Male socialization, in some cases, has presented to us that externalizing our internalized thoughts, somehow is understood as a discredit to our manhood. This is a common misconception. Here is the reality: how we communicate with either nonverbal or verbal communication will ultimately unfold into every aspect of the blueprint of our humanity, so we must be careful of what information we allow to influence us because input determines output.

Psalm 127:1 (KJV) states, "Except the Lord build the house, they labour in vain that build it." Note, that what God builds is eternal. The idea of building something is a construct that requires guidance. Not just any guidance, but the guidance of one who can fulfill His will, plan, and purpose for your life. Whereby the ability and creativity of who you are can give full expression. Salvation is the real purpose of redemption through Christ. Ephesians 2:10 (KJV) states that "we are his workmanship, created in Christ Jesus unto good works." If you have a wrong understanding of the creator, you will also have the wrong understanding of what he intends to build through you. From a human vantage point and the environment around us, we can easily perceive this message in Psalm as material or apply it in a temporal capacity. People want the Gospel to give them money or houses when the purpure and intent is to win souls.

Of course, as it relates to temporal things, acquired by men, guidance is also required.

"As I look out of the window of life I see, only the things

that surround just me, but in a distant place, there is another man, who sees things differently from his own view span. You see, we perceive to behold the things unknown, to gaze from another, but everyone has his own perception." Perception by Stephen B. Wright

When you look around the world and get a glimpse into different cultures, you will quickly discover that customs are different, so of course, guidance looks different. The actions and responses are different. What is a norm for one seems very abnormal for another. There is not always a right or wrong, it just indicates that we are subject to the influence under which we grew up, so we must be careful not to delegitimize someone else's experience, simply because it does not look like ours. I pray *Man Cave Under Construction* is a transferable source and can be instrumental within the contexts of other male cultures.

In summary, all information we receive early on was like an algorithm that reinforced our belief system. An algorithm in social media works to draw in content relevant to you based on your profile, and we subscribe to familiarity. Here is the idea: all constructs come from some influence that leaves an impression on your life. This range could come from family, television, social media, social circles, or experiences either good or bad. Individually or collectively, it becomes the framework for your individuality. These impressions build in you the composite of whom you will become. As a result, people seek information that supports their narrative once they have confirmed their position. Our earthly influences become a measuring stick by which we calculate life. These things may seem subtle, but they constantly paint an ideology, that if not internally resolved can lead one to embrace and employ these behaviors. Hatred, manipulation, and control are all ideologies. This could be passed down through deviant family backgrounds, politics, religion, or culture; however, our measurement as men of God is to examine our thoughts and actions in the light of the gospel, and through the guidance of the Holy Spirit, so that we are not driven by those narratives.

Genesis 3:1 (ESV), "Did God actually say?" was to attack what God said, produce doubt, twist the truth, and trigger the listener to entertain an alternative view, which gave rise to the fall in the garden. Pretext and post-text are important. Carefully examine the entire message to establish a complete thought. In scripture, the integrity of the Word is centered on the author's complete thought and original intent. As men, before we conclude a matter, we must be wise enough to evaluate the entirety of it before concluding, like a judge who carefully reads and rereads the manuscript, so that the decision made is correct. By not seeing the big picture, you can inappropriately reinforce a perspective that is inconclusive, and biased but could also influence behavior in an untruth. Seek the details, otherwise, all you have are assumptions. We can determine what is said but not always the person's intent behind the saying. Therefore, the conversation should come before accusations. In addition, we can easily become an advocate of misinformation. As Booker T. Washington wrote, "A lie doesn't become truth, wrong doesn't become right, and evil doesn't become good just because it's accepted by a majority."

I use some scripture in my book, but I want to be clear that the Bible is about salvation through Christ, and our mandate is to make disciples. However, how we manage our humanity can impact our effectiveness and mobility in this call. Sometimes the appropriate way to communicate what something is, is by communicating what it is not. If the message is switched, we can become easily deceived by what we believe to be true for our own needs, desire, or ambition. For example, if you are struggling economically, prosperity preaching can lure you down that road, and the foundation of the gospel will no longer be about Christ and salvation, but for what you can obtain based on what you heard. Be very careful not to let your emotions be fed at the expense of starving the truth. I heard an adage that said "It can mislead the persuaded for an extended period, and when prosperity does not appear, blaming God becomes the response." Simply, because they believed a twisted truth and mishandling of scripture.

We have been reduced to seed sowing with the hopes for a miracle and no discipline. Excited and full of emotions on Sunday but unequipped to handle the reality of Monday. Emotions have been entertained with no substance. The seed is the Word of God that produces souls, not big bank accounts. Everything that comes from Jesus' redemptive sacrifice is free and not a "quid pro quo." Believers are free and still live under the bondage of intimidation and guilt preached by their pastors. We must be careful about context, and not make the scripture say what it does not say. We have built messages that have taken people away from the Christ-centered message. Don't let your quest for things consume you from preaching the gospel of salvation.

"He that wins souls is wise" (Proverbs 11:30). We hope to deconstruct those things that have diluted the gospel for selfish gain. Even more so, we must be even more cautious of saying "God told me to tell you, "Because it creates an expectation for the hearer. Christ brought salvation, but the ability to acquire material things is a capacity of man. Some of the richest men on earth don't believe but understood how to build wealth. The gospel is about Christ's suffering and the glory that followed. The works of man are a product of his capacity to develop into what is required to achieve those goals he set to obtain earthly success. Man's responsibility is to seize every opportunity he has been afforded. God can, has, and is involved in our lives, so this is not to render God powerless in earthly matters, but so that man can accept his responsibility. God has granted us the capacity to expand and sustain our lives, but if we fail to use that ability, that deficiency lies with us. Be intentional. Hope is not enough. It needs direction. No one will know who you are unless you introduce yourself. This is your resume. You can pray that situations and circumstances line up, but ultimately something will be required of you. This is your demonstration. Make sure what you say lines up with what you do. The only way you can change your future is by thinking differently about your present. This book is intended to demystify and deconstruct oblivious patterns of thought and provide instructions from which to build.

From the time we are born to the time of our death, everything around us requires building. We are constantly attempting to rebuild or be restored to certain Genesis moments. In Genesis 1, everything was constructed by a word: "God said." That word was the construct of everything that existed, so the foundation of everything, as we know it, comes from a word. In the beginning, when God spoke, words were for creation before they were for communication, but even in communication, your actions should facilitate what you say and believe. I would like to reiterate what I mentioned earlier about influences and that we communicate out of what we believe. Likewise, we are often constructed and often construct based on words spoken to us or about us. We must be mindful of what comes from our mouths and words said about us that authenticate with our "amens."

We get a glimpse of how Adam thought and constructed in the likeness of God. That was God's original plan for us. Adam spoke and the animals were what he said. Our words communicate who we are, but when we don't keep them, our unkept words become the stigma that identifies us. We have heard the saying, "Sticks and stones may break my bones, but words will never hurt me." The truth is sometimes they do. Words are a paradox. They have the capacity to both build and tear down all within the confines of their usage and perception. What you hear, now, maybe be perceived as a replay of painful words you heard in the past. Somehow memories draw the line between the two. The problem is they may have two different connotations; however, it connects you to the same painful experience.

Words hurt and have killed dreams, stopped inventions, and unscripted books. Too often our full potential is lost in response to "No," "You can't do that," or "I wouldn't do that if I were you." Our capacity to build a life of meaning and faith has no limits unless we accept someone else's notion that it does. This capacity to build is not limited to race or culture, but rather to how you were taught to think. The capacity exists, but the moment you accept the boundaries that others impose on you, that capacity is stagnated by your view of yourself. Thus, if you are blinded by a cloud of doubt, you can become complacent in that place and won't even know you are there unless that cloud of understanding is removed. In other words, you can walk in darkness for so long until you excuse it as light.

This means there is a need to deconstruct and reconstruct how we think, because constructing life around us, as men, is not optional but mandatory. It involves analysis and evaluation. The strategy must override emotion; otherwise, how you feel will determine what you have the capacity to build. A mind that is stretched by the accurate realities in Christ shouldn't walk in darkness, and the man who understands his capacity in humanity shouldn't be limited by past misconstructions of it. We must understand why we must be intentional and committed, and take the initiative to build a meaningful life. This will surely maximize your success. When your internal infrastructure is properly constructed, you can design, construct, maintain, and improve the environment around you.

Constructing is at the heart of human existence and encapsulates everything from building words with letters in early childhood to building relationships as men. This call to build connects with God, who made us so we could represent His existence on Earth. In Genesis 2:15 (KJV), we read, "Then the LORD God took the man and put him in the Garden of Eden to tend and keep it." The garden was the environment Adam was required to sustain for human existence. He possessed a soul, which is an intellectual capacity, but also free will to choose. It was not God's responsibility, but Adam's. The focus word here in the text is "keep." The Hebrew word for "keep" is *Shamar*. *Shamar* means "to hedge about, guard, (generally) to protect, attend to." Adam was a perfect man, in a perfect environment, and everything he required was in the place where he was; however, his unfortunate decision altered that outcome.

Adam became the progenitor of rejection, which opened the door to sin and death. Unlike Adam, we are not created perfectly. Adam was created, but we were procreated, and we do not operate in a perfect environment. However, our sustainability still requires decisions. This begins with the progenitor of redemption, Christ. A man who is conscious of his faith does not build unconsciously in his humanity. It requires us to take care of what is given to us. This could suggest that human action is required when there are human necessities that are within human control. We must be conscious of the doors God opens and the relationships He presents in the building process. There is a purpose attached to them, even if it doesn't immediately appear clear.

History shows us that knowledge is progressive. We have all heard the cliché, "If I knew then what I know now," which indicates that the more we learn, the better equipped we become. This takes time. The more we learn, the more it sheds light on what we thought we knew. The more we expand our capacity to learn, the more we appreciate that there are opportunities to grow. Our capacity is sometimes limited by those things we did not understand. Building happens over time, even when the blueprint isn't completely clear. In many cases, Jesus poses a rhetorical question to people such as scribes, chief priests, and Pharisees saying, "Have you not read?" such as in Matthew 12:3 (KJV). In the original text of the book of Matthew, the word for "read" is the Greek "Anaginosko. " It seems to suggest reading it again because they missed the *details* in what they read. They knew the scripture but not the full understanding. Progressive knowledge could be simply getting an understanding or accurate interpretation of what you thought you knew. Whatever your pursuit in life, to gain an understanding of something, a knowledge base must be built. It is like having a new product with many benefits that you don't know exist, simply because you have not read the manual accurately for details. The aim of *Man Cave Under Construction* is to examine the details in all critical areas of human development.

This book is about revisiting and reevaluating the purpose of the man cave and the customs of the male culture. *Man Cave Under Construction* is about the reconstruction of our thought process. Through right thinking, we can come face-to-face with ourselves, and as a result, gain the ability to operate progressively in our realities as believers. This sort of thinking entails turning our focus toward God and coming to grips with our roles as men. The man cave has become known as a place of refuge, but escape cannot be an excuse for not representing His purpose on Earth. This includes a spiritual purpose as well as a physical presence. We have the chance to show that God is operating through us, not only in our walk, but in our homes, jobs, and whatever environment in which we are present. A temporary escape from the things that exist around us, if not handled carefully, can become a trap where we dwell on our insecurities and become too distracted to listen to the call of God.

You can never be of value to others until the value in you is realized, but it cannot be realized until you are either constructed or reconstructed to know who you are and why. This is done by inspecting or surveying whether the tools you are using to build meet the requirements. From tying shoes for the first time as a child to fulfilling your first professional assignment as an adult, you are only as effective as you have been taught to be, and how well you have learned what you were taught. To shed light on this thought, if you were in a medical crisis, would you prefer a doctor who graduated at the top of her class in medical school, or a person who barely made it out and is not committed to the job, to operate on you in a life-or-death surgery? Knowledge and skill will determine the trust level. We have all learned some good and bad behaviors. The first question is what the logic behind it is. The second question is whether it is transferrable information because it will be the window through which you see everything around you. Therefore, these perspectives must be thoroughly re-examined within your environment.

We must deconstruct the belief systems shaped by thoughts, traditions, broken places, and habits that have molded us over time. We need to be mindful of our beliefs, views, habits, prejudices, biases, fears, and blind spots as others look to us for guidance. These blind spots can incapacitate our ability to build and can prevent us from growing spiritually, mentally, physically, and emotionally. All existence is a construction zone, and everyone and everything require building. Subsequently, we are the building blocks that others may build from. We all can help build others, but if our foundations are poorly laid, so will theirs.

At times, we go through life unconsciously accepting what it offers, until something hits close to home and awakens us. When we first heard of coronavirus, we had no idea of the impact it would have. But since then, our lives have become wholly disrupted. The pandemic changed human behavior. Like any major pandemic, the COVID-19 outbreak exposed would have, should have, and could have scenarios. It highlighted what is important, like our families, but also the necessities, such as health and financial stability. It has had global health and economic impact, and we now realize how vulnerable we are. We can no longer take simple luxuries for granted because the landscape in which we operate has shifted. When we are not secure, we operate under a new norm of fear. This one event hit close to home, making us all realize that contingency planning is vitally important.

ANALYZING THE COST

Analyzing the Cost

> *"For which of you, intending to build ... does not sit down first and count the cost, whether he has enough to finish it"*
> *- Luke 14:28 NKJV*

Sometimes what you think you read is not what you read unless you get the pretext and post-text to establish context. So, there is a need to follow the thought pattern or even the style of the writer. For instance, metaphors, hyperbole, parables, etc. may be used. So then, "cost" here in this text may not mean cost as we understand it. It is simply there to tie two thoughts together to bring your attention to something familiar as an opportunity for a teaching moment. We see a summary of the Apostle's Paul view of cost in 2 Corinthians 11:22-27. In v.27 Jesus was talking about what it takes to follow him. The cost of discipleship, more specifically, priority and intentionality given to following Christ. To convey this message, he could have used a culmination of building knowledge of carpentry from his earthly father to witnessing an incomplete tower.

Building disciples is critical in our calling, but the principle of construction can be applied in multiple areas under the same discipline as a reality of the believer.

The idea is to be systematically consistent. For example, if you are on time for bible study, you should be on time at your job and on time for any social event that you attend. It is a consistency that is across the board. If not, it is just something you do but not something you are. A good builder seeks perfection and completeness when he builds, simply because his name is attached to it. The point here is that cost could be related to something other than what you think, such as time and resources. Money may be the least associated cost. It could be the cost of inactivity and overactivity. Cost does not always have anything to do with money, but always with what you decide. The reality of cost could range, depending on what you are building, from physical structures to relationships. In other words, your discipline in Christ should be a model for every other discipline in your life.

Man Cave Under Construction is not about building a man cave or any tangible structure. It is more about infrastructure for expanded thinking, those things required as a foundational pattern that is transferable to anything related to humanity. Karl Albrecht said, "You seldom improve quality by cutting costs, but you can often cut costs by improving quality." I worked in my father's upholstery shop when I was young, and he always stressed doing it right the first time, because if it was not done right the first time, it would have to be redone. Redoing work meant that he was no longer making money but losing it. I am now a man and can see the transferable context. Foreknowledge indicates that building principles are an important aspect of life, but you can't build without a blueprint. With that, the blueprint guidelines must be clear. It would require you to scale what you are intending to build. When building a home, you must monitor the cost of labor, concrete, lumber, and every other material required to determine what size house you can afford to build. If you desire to build something larger, you must determine a way to expand your capital to do so. As a man, the means behind our blueprint is an accumulation of the Spirit, Mind, and Body which all have a purpose.

As men, we often hide behind our status, job, and family. When God made man, He took the dust from the ground and molded it into a man. A formal process must occur that is intentional and defined by an instructional purpose. For example, when we were very young, we learned to form words, specifically nouns, and verbs, because they are essential for building a sentence. Sentences led to paragraphs, and paragraphs to stories. A similar process is required for developing men. Men are made, but unfortunately, our experiences and traditions have made us into something that needs to be deconstructed and remade. Although a male child is destined to become a man, this does not necessarily indicate that he has all the required tools to function as one. It starts with how he thinks. It would be an ignominy to live our life exhaustively as men being everything except what is needed, simply because we were unaware of what was required. This is the reason why understanding those needs is as important as the air we breathe. The contents of this book are designed to help identify what some of those may be.

There is a song I wrote entitled "Balance," which captures the intention of this book:

Not that I have already accomplished it, but one thing I seriously pray for.
That is to live every day as if it is my last day, no regrets, no heartburn from hidden sin, no unpaid debts.
Just living life in all its fullness, simply living what it nets.
- Stephen B. Wright.

The construction process requires a plan that analyzes every cost, possibility, condition, and variable, whether good, bad, or seemingly inconsequential. Some costs are known, while some are unknown. Cost is associated with all elements required to obtain a finished product. As it relates to 'the *Man Cave*', we are the intended finished product. An evaluation is necessary, which may disrupt everything you held to be true. That is a cost many are not willing to pay. One should stop and think through the process before proceeding. The added cost is associated with rethinking how you think, because it may restructure your current structure. That is tradition and those you associate with. At times we react, but the overall objective is to never make an impulsive decision because intentions have no merit if they cannot be performed to completion. The cost may be the invested time, money, and effort required to position yourself for future success. The scripture presents a model we can live by and confirms that God has a plan for us. The plan God provided is salvation, but human sustainability is based on your intentional plan, which all comes at a cost.

From a human perspective, no one wants to waste time or money on something that is deemed impossible to finish with the available resources. We must always consider unexpected variables. The primary focus of being responsible is on planning for the unexpected. Life circumstances have a way to un-plan what we plan. At times, the cost of being unprepared cannot be recuperated.

DECONSTRUCTION

If you observe closely Genesis chapter 3, you will discover what was maybe Adam's inner complexity. First, it appears he surrenders his leadership, and secondly, he participates in disobedience which implies that the desire of Eve was possibly Adams's desire also. The Fall that occurred in the Garden of Eden is the result of Adam's disobedience, which led to an absence of God. The tree of the knowledge of good and evil serves as a typology of desire or man's will, and Adam and Eve's actions served as a rejection of God's original instruction to Adam. Likewise, for us, sin is a rejection of God's gift of Christ and the cost he paid for us. What the serpent proposed to Eve and Adam was a pattern of thinking that disrupted what God intended. Jesus is what Adam would have looked like if he had not sinned, but unfortunately, his actions required reconstruction for all mankind. Deconstruction is the analysis of what led to that rejection. Those familiar with construction know that during the assessment of a building, remodeling a structure can be just as costly as building one from the ground up. That cost could be hidden because it is behind what cannot be seen. Whether to rebuild or not to rebuild, becomes the question. The worst mistake a builder could make is to see something that needs to be deconstructed for repair but cover it up as if it doesn't exist.

One must assess the foundation on which one builds or what has been built in one. Earlier, an analogy of algorithms was used to describe how we sometimes subscribe to a pattern of thinking without awareness. It is based on the surroundings we are exposed to. At times, it is necessary to unlearn or deconstruct what we have learned because the foundation of that knowledge cannot support what needs to be correctly built. This is true if it is not transferable or relatable information. This means the old man with his associated old thoughts and actions must be demolished. In other words, we must be transformed. If you have tried to build your life based on your status, accolades, education, and so on, then your building has been built in vain.

In his book *The Rainmaker*, John Grisham tells the story of an initially moral attorney who crosses the line into deception, and eventually, the line between right and wrong disappears. This suggests that if you interact with an idea or concept long enough, it becomes a new norm. The pattern of sin is the same. I once heard the saying, "Sin takes you further than you want to go, keeps you longer than you wish to stay, and costs you far more than you are willing to pay." The misinformation that has been passed to us, coupled with the consequences of lifestyle changes and revised laws that we now accept, will become our grandchildren's code of conviction, as it will be the only thing they know. The reality is that you can't unlearn what you know until you understand the truth about what you know, which is exactly what we must do. This concept is called deconstruction.

To deconstruct means "to take apart or examine (something) to reveal the basis or composition, often to expose biases, flaws, or inconsistencies" (Merriam-Webster, 2021). During this process, identifying who you are or, more importantly, why you are who you are is vital. Essentially, we must investigate our histories to find out why we do what we do, and even more so, why we believe what we believe. Unknowingly, we carry habits, behaviors, and biases associated with our beliefs. These customs and manners have shaped us, whether they have merit or not. In many cases, we do what we have seen others do but have no understanding of why they started doing those things in the first place. As men, we act and respond because of what we were taught, either in words, observations, or actions. As a result, we have inherited a set of imperfect rules that guide us for better or for worse.

We are all shaped by our experiences, and these experiences impact our perspectives of the world. What a person has become might, in certain instances, be the direct result of deep pain, such as abuse, neglect, or abandonment. Our understanding of ourselves and the world impacts how we approach life, but this is true for others as well. We can't simply deny other people's perspectives just because they look different than ours. By looking from different angles, you gain a more complete view, so we comprehend from the window of who, what, where, when, and how to gain a more comprehensive view. While some experiences are building blocks for constructing a life according to God's plan, others can be stumbling blocks that require us or others to seek outside assistance.

Frederick Douglass once said, "It is easier to build strong

children than to repair broken men." It is easier to build children because deconstruction is not required. Undoing the damage that has already been done is a challenge for broken men. Brokenness can only project brokenness because you're seeing the world through a broken lens. This means everything is distorted and whatever you attempt to build will be without stability or clear rationale. In addition, men are least likely to seek help for depression, and life-altering events because of the ego persona "I am man enough to handle it." When in fact, the problem is bigger than their manhood. At times counseling is required to get beyond some challenges.

Children are blank slates ready for construction. Adults, however, have been subject to processes and ideologies that have created patterns of behavior and thinking. If these experiences over a lifetime affect us adversely and turn us into broken men, there is much work that needs to be undone. Not only do you have to tear down the old beliefs, experiences, and expectations, you must then build new ones as a replacement. Many men carry their brokenness from childhood, and by adulthood, that brokenness is deeply embedded, making self-reconciliation far more difficult. I recall an incident with a fellow male in bible study who broke down crying after recalling what a woman said negatively about him 20 years prior. This meant he had not gotten past those words. He was broken from them.

In many cases, the outward signs of brokenness are symptoms of some element or incident from the past. The deconstruction phase is about digging deep to find the source of such pain. It is where you ought to be most honest and most vulnerable, as your success depends on uncovering or unveiling that which has been hidden or confronting that which you have suppressed. Two things commonly occur in situations of pain: projection of that pain onto others or isolation from people who seek to help you heal. It is like living in an uninhabitable home, but you refuse to demolish it because you have become comfortable living in its conditions. This can become the onset of a developing mental illness because one can be conforming to unhealthy thinking. Until you receive clarity and incontrovertible evidence that it is unsuitable, you may be unaware a problem exists. Demolition can create space to build a new house (man). Some real dilemmas within a man will need to be deconstructed and changed, and we will see this clearly as we move forward throughout this book. We will review these things during deconstruction and again after reconstruction.

What Happened to Man?

Silence

What led to silence?

Plato said "We can easily forgive a child when he is afraid of the dark. The real tragedy is when men are afraid of the light." This allegory speaks to what light represents. It was Adam's rejection of truth that caused his silence and the reality of our darkest truth that leads to ours. Genesis 3:9 (NIV) "But the Lord God called to the man "Where are you", this implies a pattern of normal interactions had been broken. An admission of guilt. It is sort of like a friend you speak to regularly borrows money but goes silent when the payback day arrives. Adam went silent.

The Bible does not present a minute-by-minute timeline from the Fall to when Adam spoke again. Some of us are men who went silent as boys, and we never fully regained our voice. It could be a combination of things that causes man to withdraw from speaking. Sometimes this happens because of some experience that robs a man of his voice, such as being placed in a compromising position where his inadequacies are exposed. It is better to speak up in the required moment than to live agitated by a silent past. Silence can be replicated in our actions, responses, and our overall way of thinking. Have you lost your voice? How long has it been since you lost it? Who or what silenced the adequacy in you? You must go back to that place and get closure so that your voice is recovered. You must talk about what you don't want to talk about.

The man cave mentality starts from childhood. The ability to speak has universal application. It is the confidence to communicate your thoughts, but also the freedom from hiding unnecessary burdens. We were socialized to avoid dealing with certain things, and at some point, we lose the ability to communicate how those things affect us. The greater burden for man is hiding what he feels because if revealed, he thinks it makes him less than a man. Our voices reveal our confidence and our masculinity. Silence is not what God intended; rather, it is something we have accepted as a norm.

When you become and remain silent, you grant permission to the pattern of thinking that has kept you there, and the result becomes silent frustration. In the case of Adam, his failure to follow God's instruction caused him to lose his voice and become plagued by silent frustrations.

He covered himself with fig leaves, signifying his failures and exposing his insecurities. He never understood flaws until he sinned against God. For many, falling silent might not have anything to do with a sin they committed. It could be a sin against them or some experience that left them trapped in their past.

To gain your voice, you must deconstruct who or what has made you silent in the first place. What strikes the core of manhood is shame or a feeling of being incapable of meeting a need that's expected of you. Has something emasculated you such that silence has become a way to protect a certain idea of yourself? Silence is more about what you think or how you think of yourself than how others think of you. Here is one way to find peace. Never read into anything you think a person is saying or doing unto you because you may be creating in your head ideas you have no knowledge of. Even if they do, it is their burden, not yours. Secondly, never conclude everything is about you. By this, you are not consumed by any attention given.

The capacity to become you is already in you. You are creative, chosen by purpose, but unfortunately, we end up conforming to look like and act like others. In the process, our full potential is sometimes lost in this societal pressure to conform. It's easy to listen to society's accusations of being too small, too slow, not big enough, or smart enough. Conceding, for some, is the "path of least resistance." How often are we limited by the pattern of thinking others have drawn for us, keeping us from seeing the life plan God had drawn for ourselves? Our capacity to build a life of meaning and faith has no limits unless we accept someone else's notion that it does. A man must be confident enough to acknowledge his own identity in Christ and not let society define him as something he is not. The willingness to be constrained turns silent boys into silent men, husbands, and fathers. Some incidents can leave you feeling awkward, like an outcast, or if it is your fault without an outlet to communicate your fears and anxieties. My wife and I have counseled those who have been both abandoned and molested, and how that was projected in their relationships. The good news is, that we have seen them face their challenges and received freedom and healing. You don't have to let someone else's corrupt behavior define you.

An unusual visit provoked an interesting view of a man that had an infirmity in the 5th chapter of John. "When Jesus saw him lying there and knew that he already had been in that condition for a long time, He said to him, 'Do you want to be made well?'(John 5:6 NKJV). The man in the verse was complacent and had become comfortable where he was. Like silence, complacency can become a norm, preventing progress in life. The man in the verse had become hopeless even though he always had a choice. With every question, there must be an intentional answer. It is only with the intent that you can permit yourself to change. There had to be a corresponding act that confirmed that he wanted to be made whole. Your sickness could be related to what you've been holding in. The man Jesus addressed replied that he had no one to help him. Could the issue have been with this man's thinking? Are we looking for a quick fix instead of being willing to go through the process? The process could take an instant or be a long and

drawn-out episode. Some may say they want to be well, but the truth is they become comfortable with the condition of failure, seeking handouts instead of attempting to develop independence. It takes an inspired word to reshape the way you think about where and who you are.

Distractions

> "Then the serpent said to the woman, 'You will not surely die. For God knows that in the day you eat of it your eyes will be opened, and you will be like God, knowing good and evil" (Genesis 3:4-5 NKJV).

A couple of things should be noted about this verse. First, Adam was God's creation, such the devil could not give what God had not already given. Adam forfeited it. For us, this means that the moment we accept Christ, we take on the image of God, for in Colossians 1:15 (NLT) Christ is the visible image of the invisible God. However, Adam and Eve's quest after the serpent's suggestions led to his demise, because in doing so, he broke his relationship with God.

According to Wikipedia, the free encyclopedia:

> The Hebrew word "Nahash" is used to identify the serpent that appears in Genesis 3:1, in the Garden of Eden. In Genesis, the serpent is portrayed as a deceptive creature or trickster, who promotes as good what God had forbidden, and shows particular cunning in its deception."

The author's use of the image of the venomous "serpent" and his conversation symbolized the poisoning of the mind. He poisons by advertising his version of the truth. Be careful not to be deceived by what the serpent advertises. Like Adam, if we are not cautious, visual constructs can be disguised in a dichotomy, and the obvious deception can be perceived as truth. It can be hidden within your desires, which can impact how a man both thinks and responds. James explains how this comes to fruition. James 1:13-15 (NLT) And remember, when you are being tempted, do not say, "God is tempting me." God is never tempted to do wrong,[a] and he never tempts anyone else. [14] Temptation comes from our own desires, which entice us and drag us away. [15] These desires give birth to sinful actions. And when sin is allowed to grow, it gives birth to death.

We live in a culture that resembles the tactics of the serpent. Today, millions of dollars are spent on advertising because it impacts the way we shop, what we view, and influences what we consider to be beautiful, successful, good, and bad. This advertising, much like the serpent, pushes us to adopt a false understanding of ourselves and our place in the world. When you buy into it, those who view you will validate the presented perspective in their actions toward you.

We must remain conscious of the tactics of the enemy to build our resistance against them. Manhood has been diluted with selfish ambitions and distractions that veil God's truth. The serpent offered Adam and Eve knowledge and, with it, a sense of power. There are many avenues by which a man can gain a sense of power, be it position, status, or anything that makes a person feel glorified. But with power comes arrogance. When powerful, many men become unteachable and unreachable and act as though they are untouchable. Power in the hands of the wrong person is destructive.

The tree symbolized a distraction to both Adam and Eve. Was Adam just as curious as Eve, or was he distracted by Eve? *"She took of its fruit and ate. She also gave to her husband with her, and he ate"* (Genesis 3:6 NKJV). This is an interesting topic, because Adam was with her and ate, but did Adam not notice the serpent? Did the serpent poison Eve's mind or seduce her thinking? Was Adam clueless about this event? Did he simply partake because his wife offered or suggested it to him?

The serpent created a scenario that sparked Adam and Eve's curiosity and created an appetite that exposed them to something they shouldn't have been exposed to, death. It was the presentation that caused them to reject God's plan. Many often blame Eve for humanity's Fall, but the real blame rests with Adam. Eve only heard about the tree second-hand from Adam, who received information directly from God. Eve may have thought that Adam heard God's command incorrectly, but Adam could have corrected this situation based on what he knew he heard from God. This points to an intriguing aspect of Adam, as it appears that he may have used Eve as a scapegoat. The verses speak of wanting something other than what God had already given, and Eve was Adam's way to justify this to himself. Unlike Adam, you must be sober-minded because the enemy is familiar with your weaknesses and knows exactly what to present to tempt you. Remember that when God sends an assignment, the enemy sends a distraction to abort the mission. Each one of us was formed with a purpose, and the enemy has targeted us to prevent that purpose from being fulfilled.

Altered Thinking

"The thief does not come except to steal, and to kill, and to destroy" (John 10:10 NKJV). The context is an analogy surrounding shepherding. What is being heard, who is the presenter, and what are the intentions? It is clear what the enemy's intentions are from this passage: to produce a pattern of thinking that ultimately leads to destruction. The enemy does not have the authority to kill you, but because of our free will, he does have the ability to deceive us and prompt self-destruction. He is tactical in his approach because he always uses an element of truth to sway our thinking. I call him the truth fabricator because of his ability to alter our attention away from the truth and toward a false narrative. We must be careful about listening to any and everyone who seems to be a carrier of truth. They must be examined through the light of Christ through sound doctrine.

In Genesis 3 (NKJV), Adam and Eve experienced a mindset shift that led to the destructive nature of mankind and the loss of their identity with God. This means they were God's creation; however, their actions represented the likeness of the Devil. The serpent used what God said against them so they would think God was withholding something vital from them. He gave them the impression that he cared more about their interests than God. The enemy introduced them to a pattern of thinking that was contrary to God's purpose. The altered thinking represents man's descent from God's fullness. They sought to gain, but instead, they lost.

Sin

Sin was, and remains, the enemy of purpose. Because of sin, we required reconstruction. Christ came to restore those things, and this clearly illustrates why it is very important to seek the Kingdom of God. Graeme Goldsworthy references the Kingdom of God as "God's people, in God's place, under God's rule." Many people, like the Pharisees in the New Testament, seek a literal, material kingdom. But Jesus references the "Kingdom of God within," which refers to a spiritual place, not a material one. In the Bible, the Pharisees did not recognize Jesus for who He was. Our acceptance of Christ as savior reinstitutes our relationship with the Father and the Holy Spirit residing within us; thus, the Kingdom is within. Everything that is connected to God, we have access to, and what Christ did alone direct us back to the fullness of His original intent for man. But the enemy has different plans and presents us with distractions—sin—from every angle. Therefore, it is crucial to transform the mind.

We were designed to operate in His likeness and embrace spiritual mindedness. We must deconstruct what we know and how we have come to understand what we know. Otherwise, we can be limited or bound by what we know. Our culture, experiences, and life interactions don't always teach us all we need to know, and as a result, we are subjected to fallibility. In some cases, we learn to circumvent rather than face our challenges head-on. We have to decipher our customs, so we can understand why we think the way we do. Our traditions can limit our ability to function in His likeness. Division and separation, which were created by man, limit our ability to love one another without prejudice. Instead of finding the greater you, you settle for the lesser you. Nonetheless, we must declutter and deconstruct what we think to restore our thinking to the likeness of God.

Christ wants our spiritual selves to flourish so that the best of ourselves is revealed mentally, physically, and emotionally. Remember, God is a spirit (John 4:24 KJV), and that represents your likeness to Him because His spirit resides in us as believers. God is so much greater than our material views of life. The problem occurs when we reframe our humanity to include God rather than becoming spiritual men who embrace their humanity. We are often drawn into man-made traditions and then call them God. You don't build a house first and then try to add a foundation. Christ is the only sustainable foundation.

What Kind of Manager Are You?

> Proverbs 15:22 (AMP) "Without consultation *and* wise advice, plans are frustrated, but with many counselors, they are established and succeed."

How you manage things around you, becomes the premise of a consequence or a reward. Deconstruction or unlearning is necessary before you start building again as the manager of your project—you. Adam's role was to manage God's plan in the garden (the project), just like we are to manage or exhibit stewardship over what God has placed in our care. Adam was given an assignment. Times have changed from the time of Adam; however, the assignment of our times consists of nurturing our relationship with Him. Previously, Adam went silent, which indicated he choose to disconnect from his source. God to us is abba Father, our source. As men in humanity, we are responsible for our families, friends, health, and finances. We can't expect God to do what He expects of us. For example, you must go to work to take care of your family, and you must communicate to resolve any issues that may occur. There should be a clear line of demarcation between waiting for something to happen and putting in the effort to make it happen. Some things are not prayer points, because within you is the ability to resolve them. The only disclaimer is that you cannot let your pursuit of material accomplishments compromises the value of relationships you've formed, because after success has been achieved, valuable relationships are all that are left. No matter how remarkable the achievement is, you can't recover the special moments missed and the relationships sacrificed in the process.

Real success, therefore, is proven by how well you manage what is in your care—and relationships are the first things we should learn to manage. Our deconstructed experiences, cultural norms, and traditions become the tools we use to build a life we can be proud of. Even our mistakes provide wisdom if we are self-reflective students. From this, I would like to present three types of managers, but it will be up to you to decide the type of manager you want to be.

The Purposeful Manager

The purposeful manager is both a visionary and a planner. The first aspect of building should be spiritual because it is God's purpose, plan, and will for man. However, he must also build within his human experience. He must grow spiritually while also managing his earthly responsibilities. He sees what lies ahead even before it is manifested into being. Therefore, he plans and prepares for the process of building through to the manifestation of the finished work. He is also a time manager. This manager does not waste time being idle or distracted because he is focused on accomplishing the results, even if that means eliminating close relationships that become distractions. It is not that he does not have time for anything else, he just knows that time is of great importance in achieving his aim. He knows that one small distraction can disrupt the build of a lifetime, and he understands that the ultimate goal of the enemy is to present something that appeals to him. His tactic is for man's works to go incomplete, but due to spiritual discernment, he recognizes the distraction when it appears. This means the measurement is in light of God's word.

The most important factor in any build is the awareness that you are building on a solid foundation. In the same way that builders use concrete and depth when building structures, Christ is the foundation in building everything that is connected to your purpose. Building a vertical relationship with God helps to build horizontal relationships with those you will encounter on your journey. The vertical relationship deals with growing in the knowledge of Him, which leads to horizontal relationships that build others in Christ. In this, you will understand that no encounter is coincidental and that there is a reason even if we don't understand the why and how. When you represent Christ daily, you become an example of "I planted, Apollos watered, but God gave the increase" (1 Corinthians 3:6-8 NKJV).

On the other hand, it may simply be a temporary lesson of growth or perseverance. Even your trials reaffirm that you are in the hands of the potter, as God presents you with opportunities to form life in His image. Always be prepared for God to use you whenever He deems fit. "Be diligent to present yourself approved to God, a worker who does not need to be ashamed, rightly dividing the word of truth" (2 Timothy 2:15 NKJV). Ministry, family, business, etc. all correlate to purpose. The purposeful manager's dedication and commitment are to fulfill God's will with the understanding of being a good steward of spiritual, physical, mental, and emotional necessities.

The Careless Manager

> "But anyone who hears my teaching and doesn't obey it is foolish, like a person who builds a house on sand. 27 When the rains and floods come and the winds beat against that house, it will collapse with a mighty crash" (Matthew 7:26-27 NLT).

This manager always acts first and thinks later, and as such, his circumstances dictate his build. He quickly becomes counterproductive, like a dog chasing its tail or a businessman never getting work done because he is constantly fixing what he did not do right the first time. He is always behind schedule and lacks resources. A good example is a man who takes a new wife and then looks for a job. He never thinks of doing the reverse. The only driving force is the wife, which indicates he has no regard for himself or herself. He lives as if there is no tomorrow.

In some circumstances, living this way may seem to work, but when the manager's progress is dependent on following a process or procedure, then it is not. Without Christ, he will never be stable and will be double-minded due to his inability to think through processes.

He lives off spontaneity as if to say everything will work itself out, and in the process, he works himself into a never-ending jam, while blaming God for his misfortune. As it relates to the above text, it is because he is disobedient to the word or plan of God. He also lacks order and everything in his life is out of balance. His walk with God is nonexistent until he is overwhelmed with the failures he has created. There is a domino effect that affects his spiritual, physical, mental, and emotional well-being.

The Selfish Manager

"4Love suffers long and is kind; love does not envy; love does not parade itself, is not puffed up; 5 does not behave rudely, does not

seek its own, is not provoked, thinks no evil"
(1 Corinthians 13:4-5 NKJV).

We can all find ourselves here and not realize it. A selfish manager violates all the rules of love because he never considers the thoughts or feelings of anyone but himself. The Love of Christ **serves**, but that of a selfish manager's thought process is so twisted that he thinks everything revolves around him, so he takes. He communicates as if no one else has a voice and emphasizes both verbally and by action that their opinions don't matter.

He has a self-centered personality that prevents him from being empathetic or sympathetic toward others. This person builds with no one but himself in mind. This means he will steal someone else's plans and resources so that he can get the credit. He is a coveter and is never satisfied. He is capable of slandering others to uplift his interests. He is arrogant, a taker, and feels entitled. Everyone, in his mind, owes him something. His only intention is to meet his physical, mental, and emotional needs, and spiritually, he is his god.

You must re-evaluate yourself considering these managers to build the best view of yourself in light of Christ. As a manager, every man has a role in humanity, and the ability to determine which is God's and which is man's role is vitally important. With knowledge, you understand the impact and influence you have in determining the outcome of everything you manage. The product at completion will be a composite of how you think. It is interesting to note that no matter what type of manager you are, you can be so busy building that you neglect the things that matter the most, such as your health, your finances, and even your family. It takes evaluation and balance. The final question would be: is all that you built worth all that was expensed?

Introspection

Where Are You Spiritually?

"Then the Lord God called to the man, 'Where are you?'" (Genesis 3:9 NLT).

After Adam partook in what Eve shared, God, asked Adam, "Where are you?" This was a rhetorical question because God already knew where Adam was and the circumstance and details surrounding it. The observation in this verse is twofold. Adam had left the place where he was. In a sense, he was physically present but spiritually absent. In context, his actions caused a separation between himself and God. He knew it and was aware that God knew it also. In principle, our actions often separate us and misalign us with what we are responsible for. Adam was responsible for what God said to him; therefore, he neglected his responsibility to his wife as being head, and his relationship with God. Instead of being accountable, he blamed Eve. This responsibility has everything to do with his relationship with God, but their willingness to entertain the enemy convinced him and his wife to consider another option. Even though this is recorded as Adam's experience, we must also be mindful of the craftiness of words that present distractions to us also.

If a troubled relationship is of any value, there should be instinctive attempts to try to repair it before it is abandoned. From the beginning of time, God has always set out to repair His relationship with a man (humanity). He did it for us through the redemptive work on the cross. It is not that God didn't know where Adam was. He was aware of where he was because there is nothing hidden from Him. It was for that very reason Adam had attempted to hide from Him. It was as if to say, "I am trying to run away from who I was in the plan, purpose, and will of God." Like any situation of guilt, you avoid being seen by those who are aware of the truth.

Sin's shamefulness causes us to run into isolation, which makes us avoid God instead of accepting His grace. In the case of Adam, sin symbolized that the fellowship between the Creator and His creation had been broken. Since the creation of man, God had been in constant fellowship with Adam. This fellowship may have indicated that God missed fellowshipping and was disappointed that Adam responded as if he was denying the fact that a relationship ever existed—the very core of rejection. Have you ever done something and tried to hide from God? Have you ever wondered what would have happened if Adam had gone to God and admitted his mistake? To man up and take ownership would have been his first step in attempting to reconcile the relationship. To shed light, despite man's disobedience, it is God who seeks to reconcile us to himself.

Adam may have been disappointed in his failure and was afraid of how God would respond. This highlights our basic human frailty. You are not perfect, so don't pretend to be. Duplicity only teaches you to cover up those things you need to address. This act of covering up only leads to isolation and a pattern of behaviors leading to more cover-ups. Transparency means you have nothing to hide and can be held accountable for every action you take. We'll never know with any kind of certainty what God's response would've been if Adam had been honest instead of blaming Eve; however, we will discover through the discourse of this book that God is merciful.

The truth about hiding is that it taints communication. The moment silence is conceived, the process of alienation begins. This either leads to no communication or communication on a need-to-know basis. This applies to our relationships with both God and with others—that is, we only talk to God when we are in need, and that same agenda applies to our relationships with our human counterparts. It is vital to understand the crux of the man cave mentality that Adam experienced, so we can learn from it.

Where Are You Physically?

"Recognizing and preventing men's health problems is not just a man's issue. Because of its impact on wives, mothers, daughters, and sisters, men's health is truly a family issue."- Bill Richardson-

Your neglect can lead to a quality-of-life issue which would create a burden requiring someone to take care of you. If you die prematurely, it also leaves heavy hearts, especially when it could have been prevented. Don't ever have the regret of looking back and saying I wish I had done things differently.

"For He knows our frame; He remembers that we are dust" (Psalm 103:14 NKJV).

This gives light to the reality of what dust signifies in the state of mortality. That is our humanity. We are susceptible to the things that are present on Earth. Being aware of our humanity presents the argument that we are not invincible in this flesh and are subject to disappointment, sickness, failures, and consequently to the choices we make. At times, we tend to take life for granted. At times, we live as if things will sustain or maintain themselves. We must use methods of prevention and preservation to sustain our welfare. At times, one of the most neglected aspects of man is his health. Whether it is from the thoughts of invincibility or the influences of the "suck it up or shake it off" socialized view playing out in an adult reality, the fact is health is compromised.

Our health and well-being are also important. We eat carelessly, yet we expect God to heal or keep us healthy. He could heal, but what would be the lesson gained? We are aware that death is inevitable, but our actions can lead to premature death. We look at generations before us and we eat what they passed down as traditions and customs; however, some of what they ate was because they weren't aware of the danger or could not afford to eat healthier. Much of what we eat is by choice, although it may be killing us slowly. Think of it genetically: we inherited certain diseases through the DNA of our parents. This means for those who are yet to have kids, you have the potential to pass down health issues you inherited and what you acquire to your kids. It does not make their future look so bright, does it? In addition, drinking and smoking long-term can put you at risk of heart disease and stroke. Heart disease is the leading cause of death in both men and women. We can't control genetics but eating habits and exercise we can. Our stewardship over this body means that we need to take care of what God has entrusted us with. I am not saying you shouldn't drink, but make note of its cause and effect.

Our physical nature on Earth, as we know it, is designed to be both temporary and conditional. Job states, "Man that is born of a woman is of few days" (Job 14:1 NKJ), which means that because of the sin of Adam, our bodies will diminish, and we are destined to die a physical death. "The prudent see danger and take refuge, but the simple keep going and pay the penalty" (Proverbs 27:12 NIV). These writings were observations of human experiences. Just like the way that what we listen to can affect our thinking, what we eat or do can affect our bodies as well. This means our actions can determine our quality of life.

Tim Green is a former NFL linebacker who was diagnosed with amyotrophic lateral sclerosis (ALS). He acknowledged that the multiple blows to the head, concussions, and hits he gave and received probably contributed to his diagnosis, but the excitement of playing football causes you to never consider your future well-being. This is a paraphrase, and there is no evidence to link it to ALS, but football concussions have been linked to other debilitating health issues. I love watching football, but it is a brutal sport, and we have heard stories about the quality of life after the game. I too suffered a career-ending football injury in high school. This simply means that we are not invincible, and we do have a choice to accept, mitigate, or risk a certain quality of life. I have two torn rotator cuffs and have had knee surgery and have come to understand that I am limited in what I can do because of it. This is just one example, but there are so many other aspects to our physical well-being that place us in danger, such as the foods we eat, the people we entertain, and various lifestyle choices we make. All of these can contribute to the demise of our physical health. For example, if I were in a gang that had shoot-outs daily, my life expectancy would be greatly shortened due to my activities.

Our bodies often speak to us, signaling when something is wrong. It is our choice to find out what our bodies are saying. Our responsibility is to consult with someone who possesses the knowledge and expertise in the areas we do not have adequate knowledge. One night, my brother felt an enormous pain in his side. He had decided to sleep through the pain but was led to drive himself to the hospital, where they discovered a blood clot in his lungs. He was informed that had he not come in when he did, he would have died. Have you ever felt a conviction so strong that you knew it was in your best interest to take heed, but stubbornness caused you to face a consequence that could have been prevented? In addition to the common male trait of avoiding doctors, or rather not knowing, we are also hindered because of the financial cost that may be incurred, so we default to the "man up and shake it off" philosophy we were taught as kids. I recall attending a funeral, and a friend on the deceased behalf began by saying, "I don't know whether to be sad or angry." This was because the deceased person had refused to go to the doctor, and when it came to the point the pain was unbearable, he was discovered to be in stage four cancer after finally being checked out. Early detection may have saved his life.

As men, we often have a phobia of going to the doctor because of our perception of manhood. Then, when it is too late, we fight to cling to life because we ignored that which could have been prevented. Having regular doctor visits could have identified and treated what had seemingly become untreatable. Our physical health deteriorates primarily due to poor diet and no exercise. However, there are some things that we are genetically predisposed to. So, knowing your family history is equally important.

Wayne Dash exclaimed, "We've all heard exercise helps you live longer. But a new study goes one step further, finding that a sedentary (inactive) lifestyle is worse for your health than smoking, diabetes, and heart disease." We have become increasingly more lethargic with the emergence of online shopping and gadgets that have decreased our physical activity and critical thinking. We can get everything we need at the click of a finger without leaving our comfort zones. Additionally, our smartphones, which are great in some ways, have made us simple-minded, because they do our thinking for us. From remembering phone numbers to researching data, it does the research for us, so we use less of our brain muscles, memory, and cognitive processing. We are creating a new norm of laziness, which is leading to the demise of our physical and **Mental health.**

Often, we hear the slang "It is what it is", which is to say that's just a part of life. However, how it affects people personally and mentally raises a harsh reality. Mental illness is a greater issue than we can ever imagine, and what is even more frightening is that we allow the view of manhood to become the stronghold that prevents us from seeking necessary help. Some of us were constructed in some ways to become the apprentice of self-destruction.

One of the more common conditions of mental illness is depression. As Jane Leonard wrote, "Depression is almost twice as common in women as men. However, men are far less like than women to seek treatment for it." This narrative seems to solidify the characteristics of the man cave culture. How you manage things around you, becomes the premise of either a consequence or reward.

According to the Mayo Clinic, "about 1 in 5 adults has a mental illness in any given year. Some are hereditary and are passed down through genetics. However, it could be created by circumstances and situations we face in life. Traumatic experiences such as military combat or assault are contributors. Exposure to certain lifestyles, such as alcohol excess and recreational drugs are risk factors". We probably know friends and family who have either been divorced or lost loved ones that have never been the same since. We, at times, brush it off without understanding the impact of what they are dealing with or how they will respond to it. What we, sometimes, chalk up as life, such as losing a house in foreclosure, or a job, others are severely impacted. For some, the impacts are compounded and are the results of early childhood experiences such as abandonment, neglect, or abuse. This culmination becomes the "straw that breaks the camel's back." With a rise in social media content, how a person responds socially to one's content can lead to a person's depression. Mental Health is important because during these experiences a person can become a danger to themselves and even others. Your attention to detail and courtesy to others can be someone's saving grace. The idea is to remind others that they don't have to face their challenge alone.

Sexual Health

This segment is no means to promote sex, but it is a vital part of your humanity. A healthy mind equals a healthy body in most cases. For one, a healthy mind makes healthy decisions. Some of our sexual issues are the result of those decisions. Mancave culture is a thought pattern that is sometimes independent of those who need to be involved. As men, we know we are also sexual creatures who sometimes forsake our health in that capacity. Dr. Newton, a urologist with Unity Point Health, says, "You might be surprised by how many men have erectile dysfunction." He says it affects about 50 percent of men over the age of 40 and is even more common as men age. Two of the most common causes are heart disease and diabetes, according to the Mayo Clinic. This could be the result of poor upkeep of physical health.

In other instances, we can become our own worst enemy. If we are not careful, we can even identify with both the careless and selfish builders. I, like many others, have used sex for self-fulfillment by totally disregarding rationality and the word of God at that moment. Many careless behaviors can and have led to procreation we did not plan for, or to the transmission of embarrassing sexually transmitted diseases. Therefore, I think marriage is the only appropriate stance for sex. In my book *The*

Other Side of You, I explain why. This is the reason why we must rethink the notion of manhood.

In an article published in *Psychology Today* entitled "Poor Judgment? Decision-Making and Sexual Arousal" (Shelton, 2013), Shelton confirms the old cliché that "men think with the wrong head." It states the tunnel vision of arousal allows temporary denial of consequences. Sexual arousal, in sum, hijacks the brain leading to a focus on immediate pleasure and gratification. Typically, after ejaculation occurs, a male then begins to consider (and often worry about) the consequences of his sexual involvement.

This is nothing new, as David demonstrated this through his interest in Bathsheba in 2 Samuel 11. He saw her bathing and stopped at nothing to have her, even though she was married. He even placed her husband on the front line to be killed just to fulfill his lust and desires.

What lengths have you gone to for sex? How many women have you lied to by saying "I love you" and going through the process of dating just to have sex? The consequences of sex to your health, including your sanity and well-being, can become a stumbling block in maximizing your full potential. But more importantly, have you ever considered what impact that behavior has on the women you deceive? Your actions can leave emotional, mental, and physical damage on a person that lingers long after your fulfillment. It has produced children outside the marriage and burdens that you can never outlive. Only when you allow the leading of the spirit, wisdom, and discipline we you be steered away from such traps.

In that moment of sexual passion, we are driven to

get a release, but it is not until after we are done that, we evaluate our actions, often realizing that we regret them. Seeing something sexual like pornography can open us up to an instant appetite for sex. Like a chemical addiction, your body chases a high that it cannot chemically and biologically reproduce. It creates an appetite for sexual experiences that can't be reproduced in the bedroom, creating disappointment when that expectation can't be met. The enticement keeps you chasing the memory of what you have previously seen and envisioned. This switch can turn on quickly, but it's difficult to turn it back off again. This can lead to unguarded decisions.

If you are in an environment where sex is offered and you have no self-control, you risk making a bad decision. Avoiding certain environments is critical to our survival. For many men, paying to keep the lights on might come second to buying a woman a gift that might lead to sex. This sounds pretty foolish when we're not in a sexual frenzy. We are sometimes noted for thinking and making wrong decisions, which is why it is critically important to guard your mind.

Where Are You Financially?

Even though many of us have been taught that men are providers, many have taken an approach of responding, rather than thinking ahead. Early and often, we are drawn into patterns of thought that were created through either proactive or reactive thinking. If proactive, you are on the right path, but reactive is when circumstances become your building blocks. In this, you are never prepared.

This is often seen when we adapted to some predisposed experience and is influenced by the environment we are in. We then conclude with its norms. We patterned after how we witnessed them and how they were handled. If no one in your family was familiar with investing, you may not have been privileged to get these opportunities. They may have had to spend every penny to make ends meet, simply because of how life unfolded. We are a product of what was familiar to us. We have witnessed our families struggle or heard stories of struggle that have conditioned us to view this as a norm.

In many situations, what we owe is greater than what we possess, outside of buying a home or car, which can be the exceptions. A common term that brings reality to this financial struggle is "upside down," which simply implies "in or into an inverted position." Owing a lot of money, for example, makes it difficult to make ends meet. Often, a person began creating debt a long time before they begin creating wealth. For example, without being educated, an individual gets approved for a credit card and begins to spend it as if it is their money. Minimum payments and interest rates soon consume them. They are not spending time and effort attempting to get out of a hole they dug for themselves. This often leads to a snowball effect. "Metaphorically, a snowball effect is a process that starts from an initial state of small significance and builds on itself, becoming larger, and also perhaps potentially dangerous and disastrous" (Wikipedia, 2021). The disastrous portion could be collections or high-interest payday loans in addition to ruined relationships, due to the inability to pay back family and friends.

The prosperity gospel can lead to an erroneous view of God. He is often blamed for our unsuccess. Some have come to believe it is God's duty to prosper us without any responsibility of working for ourselves. Malik Willis, said in a Pro football interview, "pray as if it is up to God, and work as if it is up to you." This sums up our responsibility. The better question to ask is, "Have I placed myself in a position to prosper and managed my finances and resources accordingly?" I am not asking if you prayed, but have you received the education or skills that will cause you to excel financially? Are you a good steward of your mind, abilities, and potential, or have you buried your gifts for handouts and miracles? If you have not used what God has given, you can't blame God. Whether you are single with the ability to prepare, or upside down trying to find a way out, we must realize that deconstruction of financial thinking comes with the cost of deconstructing our attitude and understanding of finance.

As 1 Timothy 6:10 (NLT) states, "For the love of money is the root of all kinds of evil. And some people, craving money, have wandered from their true faith and pierced themselves with many sorrows." To place this verse in context, you must first read the pretext and post-text. This is one of the most mishandled verses in the Bible. It is about those who pervert the gospel for their financial gain, like that of the prosperity gospel whereby lying, cheating, and stealing is involved. I am in no way suggesting that a laborer is not worthy of compensation, but if money is the center of the message, rather than Christ and salvation, it is another gospel. Remember, the gospel pertains to Christ's suffering and the glory that shall follow. However, money itself isn't evil. If it were, then we would have no earthly resource for survival today. In some cases, people barter, trade, or issue favors, but in industrialized communities, you can't trade for such things as electricity or homes. The key is to not exploit others for financial gain. Money is required to operate in this Earthly realm. The reality is you can't just expect money to come by just praying. It requires work, unless you are disabled, or you came upon riches by other means. In Ecclesiastes 10:19 (NKJV), we find the statement that "money answers all things." This is about money being the answer to those things having a cost. Food, shelter, etcetera, all require money, suggesting money is a necessity. We often view money as the object of the transaction, but it is sometimes seen in the intangibles such as stress, worry, and even arguments. These all are the result of the lack of money, so money would have answered these things. Therefore, money is not evil, but when used for deception, it can be. We should use it properly and always give thanks to Him who gave us the capacity to acquire it.

Where Are You Emotionally?

Men and emotions are like a taboo that would get your man card revoked in a man cave conversation. To mention "man" in the same sentence as "emotions" is like mixing oil with water; however, it does exist. We just view it in a different light and classification. To show the normalization in male cultures of the idea that emotions are a sign of weakness, Daphne Rose Kingma wrote in *The Men We Never Knew*:

"We've dismissed men as the feelingless gender—we've given up on them. Because of the way boys are socialized, their ability to deal with emotions has been systematically undermined. Men are taught, point-by-point, not to feel, not to cry, and not to find words to express themselves."

Although the intentions were meant to harden us to not fold in adversity, we weren't taught how to intelligently process the tension we felt inside.

We are the product of what we have learned, and if we defy the principles of what we learned, we think maybe something is wrong with us. This is a sort of emasculated misconception. The psychological shift, as a result, may be adaptation: when rejected, you find acceptance among others who feel rejected, when in fact, there is nothing wrong with you at all. You see, emotions are as natural as the air we breathe. Emotion is "a conscious mental reaction (such as anger or fear) subjectively experienced as a strong feeling usually directed toward a specific object and typically accompanied by physiological and behavioral changes in the body" (Merriam-Webster, 2021). It is not emotions, but the lack of understanding of emotions that is the greatest weakness. A sort of man code that has not been explained. I can imagine it was intended for toughness, to prevent us from becoming push-overs, or better yet someone using it as a sign of weakness to take advantage of you, but if not explained, it becomes a dysfunctional habit—one that may be beneficial in one aspect but is an obstruction in another. The obstruction is you can live life in a silo dealing with issues that require external help. Without that help, you can end up masking the pain through perilous means.

An interesting article that articulates how male emotions are distributed is "How to Crack the Code of Men: Feelings in Psychology," which states that:

Just because men aren't *adept* at expressing their feelings, don't for a minute think they *don't* feel and feel deeply. Many times, men express their feelings using a secret code—a code that even they can't decipher. **Men may convert one feeling into another.** Men may convert stereotypically feminine feelings, such as sadness or vulnerability, into feelings like anger or pride—feelings more socially acceptable for them to experience. (Kingma, 2014)

Sometimes we project our emotions differently and distribute them through possibly sports or sex. Often, emotions are detached and converted, as a demonstration of aggressive behaviors often inflicted upon others. We associate emotions in manhood with either toughness or self-fulfillment. Strength is associated too often with a victory rather than in processing defeat. It is narrated as present in the image of a macho personality. This means men often opt for other means of emotional release. Some claim control through assertiveness, vocal projections in relationships, or many times through sexual means. A more drastic means are using alcohol and drugs to cope with what he is internalizing. Yes, sex is a form of release, but often we don't understand ourselves or know how to share our feelings with others. Furthermore, the sexual experience had nothing to do with sex. It was a way of dealing with some other frustration, but we can end up hurting others in the process.

This is because some were not educated on other

methods of dealing with our emotions, or were too macho to consider other options. Many of us were taught that showing emotion is a sign of weakness. Yet, men sometimes go on a rampage. Emotions uncontained are like a ticking time bomb awaiting the most inopportune moment to explode. Amid a negative emotional shift, there is an even greater opportunity to make a split decision that is detrimental to yourself or others. When they are not managed, someone you love becomes the casualty of your unresolved frustration. For instance, the frustration from work can carry over to lashing out at your wife or kids. Minor frustration with them does not warrant a major blow-up due to the frustration of what you experienced on the job. These are two separate issues, which are a result of not knowing how to diffuse the range of emotions that are bottled up.

In other situations, what is not always comprehended is that the expectations of relationships affect emotions, especially if unmet or unkept expectations seem to be too difficult to manage. The effect is most common in romantic relationships. This may also contribute to why it is difficult to commit for most men, due to a combination of emotions and expectations. When what is expected of us is greater than what seems achievable, our societal understanding tells us that we are not good enough and we find it difficult to express how that makes us feel. This can lead to low self-esteem and emasculation. We wonder why a seemingly timid man suddenly and without warning snaps, or why what appears to be a perfectly normal human being puts a gun to his head and pulls the trigger. Emotions attached to a single thought are fleeting. A decision in a single moment can go either way, depending on what we give power to. We must learn to express how we feel emotionally in a healthy way rather than bottling it inside of us.

With understanding, one can conclude that you don't have to be emotional, just emotionally intelligent, emotionally present, and emotionally connected. Emotional intelligence is important, because no man wants to be deemed weak, and have his subliminal man card revoked among his peers. Therefore, it is important to understand what emotions are. Emotional intelligence is knowing how to manage your emotions. It is knowing when and where to express them. Intelligence prevents you from making emotional decisions that can lead to detrimental actions, like doing what can't be undone or saying what can't be unsaid. We noticed that the year 2020 was highly intense and emotional. Men and women were emotional; however, women are more likely to release their emotions from person to person, while a male is most capable of releasing his pent-up aggression through some unrelated activities.

A young lady asked me why it is so easy for men to walk away from a relationship while the woman carries the brunt of the emotions. It is because in most cases we are not emotionally connected, nor do we know how to be. We were taught to hide those emotions at a very young age, with the mantra "Be tough and don't cry," so while walking this rite of passage, we lost touch with understanding how to feel or what emotions were. With a clear understanding, there is a need to be emotionally connected in a romantic relationship. Even beyond this, some relationships require emotional support, such as your spouse, family, or children. Women are better at expressing their emotions in relationships. Both men and women are emotional, we just express them differently. As I mentioned earlier, men frequently displace their emotions into areas such as sports. For example, we can build anticipation for weeks ahead of a big game only to be disappointed at the outcome, which can lead to an increase in our frustration that plays out in emotional actions and responses. We have seen videos of men destroying TVs after their team lost. That is an emotional response to disappointment.

As men, we can hide our emotions to meet certain male social expectations. When a man is overwhelmed with responsibilities, he might attempt to escape his reality through fantasies with no expectations. This means he can decompress without the burden of responsibility. Most often, sex is a relief, whether it is frustration from expectations or some responsibility that require his attention. Sometimes it flows down the same stream. At times, emotional frustration has nothing to do with sex and everything to do with what we have been taught to hide, which is expressing our emotions naturally.

One day, while I was working as an Uber driver, a male passenger opened up to me. I was not sure if it was guilt or the need for another male to relate to. The first thing he said was that he worked hard for his family as if to justify where I picked him up—a strip club. I did not know or judge him, but I did ask questions to open a dialogue. It appeared that he worked very hard to provide for the desires of his family, but he was overwhelmed with keeping up with the expectations, according to the conversation. At that moment, I realized that despite our ethnic differences, we were quite similar. We have male issues, and our ways of dealing with them are sometimes the same. His frustrations quickly reminded me of my own.

You see, the reason I was an Uber driver was out of desperation and frustration. I was financially challenged and needed to make money to get out of debt and help get my son through an expensive college, all while taking on a new wife. Like the passenger, I was disappointed with where I was in life financially and overwhelmed by expectations but did not want to disappoint those who depended on me. Without knowing how to cope, we can disappoint them in different ways. For men, disappointment extends to not meeting the needs of their loved ones. This is why I tend to emphasize this book's stages, the man alone, then the wife and children. This is so we are prepared so that it can eliminate the weight of expectations. We deal with this burden differently than women even though there is always a need to release that frustration. As men, we often internalize that frustration, keeping it from being released appropriately. Could this man have civilly externalized his frustrations that his wife could understand instead of going to a strip club? Perhaps, but it depends on how they relate to and understand each other. I did not frequent strip clubs, but in the past, I looked at porn and had sexual encounters with women, not out of a need to have sex but to get a release from my frustrations.

Behind our greatest desires as men are our greatest fears, and behind our sexual defiance is our fear that our greatness will be denied. Our greatness can be as simple as having a sustainable income to meet our family's needs. At times, it is the creativity we are unsure how to release. When the stress of doing all those manly duties overwhelms us, we need a release from that frustration and insecurity, often without knowing how to obtain that. This could be why there are so many brothels and sexually explicit venues. These places have become man caves, where men can express what is on the inside in the only way we know-how. As men, we don't want anyone to know that we too have fears, insecurities, and failures, because according to what is expected, we believe that they will emasculate us. We must change that perspective. That is why understanding emotions and being able to communicate them through a healthy outlet is so important. Tied to our emotional distress are the false expectations we create knowing it may be impossible to fulfill them.

Where Are You Mentally?

> "For as he thinks in his heart, so is he. 'Eat and drink!' he says to you, but his heart is not with you" (Proverbs 23:7 NKJV).

The greatest demon we face is in how we think. Like that in any situation, the enemy presents what is desired, "But his heart is not with you." What he offers has the intent to deceive, and that becomes the distraction that poisons our minds. The things that come from it are only the byproducts. The quest for power through deception, hatred, abuse, or arrogance are ploys that the enemy uses against us.

We are said to have a 'guy code,' a set of self-prescribed rules that govern our thoughts and actions, and I've taken the liberty of merging it with the term 'conviction.' According to the Cambridge Dictionary, "Conviction is a strong belief that is not likely to change or the strong feeling that your beliefs are right. More so, it may be something you feel obligated to uphold to be considered a man." The consolidated concept means a set of rules you are convinced of the value of keeping. However, the guy code is constructed by a pattern of thinking inherited through human traditions. These traditions could be a result of someone's biases or self-imposed misconceptions. Depending on the influence, they can create their own set of convictions so powerful that they are convinced by them. Historically, we see the strong conviction aspect emanate from racial and gender inequalities. Such people emphatically believe certain things and can't be convinced otherwise. By becoming an apprentice of truth, we examine everything we know to be true, to establish whether it is so. The truth I am referring to is the rightly divided word of God. It takes deconstructing what has been ingrained through generations of practice by people we trusted until it seems justified, creating blind spots that marginalize our thinking. This invariably damages the lives of many.

We have heard "let your conscience be your guide," but your conscience can deceive you. After all, your conscience emerged from what you were taught. Those influences. I recall my dad telling stories about when he was growing up. He and his siblings were not allowed to play ball because it was considered a sin. This meant that he felt guilt whenever they played with a ball. That guilt was learned, but his conscience is what internalized the moral imperative to feel guilty because what he was taught became his moral compass. Your conscience is how you were taught to understand on autopilot, so it responds based on what you know. Therefore, you must be open to continuous learning. Otherwise, what you think you understand can be a stumbling block to internal freedom. The arduous progress of disentangling tainted thinking can take a lifetime. The challenge for men is to restructure our thinking to be that of Christ's thinking on a subject. Although some of what has been ingrained in us were influenced by good intentions, some of what we know may no longer serve our purpose or be the result of misinformation.

There are demons we don't care to talk about. We tag them as habits or justify them as simply the consequence of being a man, but seldom do we call them what they are. We expose ourselves to things that plant thoughts in our minds. We then entertain these thoughts which eventually create strongholds. We are in essence the stronghold we attribute to everyone else.

For generations, we have been linked by a common enemy through our fathers, their fathers before them, and so on. These are deeply ingrained traditions that we hold to be foundational for governing our actions. We all exhibit behaviors that have become the cultural norm, but following God means challenging these norms and changing the associated behaviors.

Behaviors are sometimes glorified until their consequences are exposed. Then we become horrified by their consequences. We can enjoy commercials that celebrate drinking until someone is killed by a drunk driver. Sexual promiscuity is fun until it damages the life of someone close to you. Abuse is washed over as a misunderstanding until someone has to live a lifetime with the mental, emotional, or physical scars of it. The behaviors we turned a blind eye to or excused have both magnified and mutated into an invisible enemy. The distractions of men have now become normalized habits, and it is up to us to change the patterns of distraction that infiltrate and influence our behaviors.

Even the church has adopted thoughts and behaviors that have become distractions to building the Kingdom. The biased position of the church has failed to bring about healing. We stare at people in our congregation who neither look nor dress like us and find ourselves asking, "Should you be here?" We have made a loving God look unloving based on our actions. We must cast out the demon by its name. We have been seduced and poisoned by the enemy disguising himself as truth. A demon forges the truth with words and follows it with deceitful actions. Even the church has purchased his bill of goods when they support it. We wonder why the children of this culture are growing more disobedient. It is because what they see is disguised as righteousness. It is time to clean up and man up by reconstructing our minds. Only the leading of the spirit and accurate teaching can bring about clarity.

Finally, one of the greatest means of deconstruction is to understand why you think the way you do. It is good to go back generations, if possible, to understand the challenges of your parents and grandparents when they were growing up. This may even include learning about the pain and brokenness that led to behaviors that shaped them. Due to their experiences and our predecessor's 'thinking', actions may have been a projection of their experiences, though not intentionally. This may shed light on how and why they thought the way they did. It could have been related to the times or some unwelcome experience. The discussion could promote healing, as talking about pain heals wounds and can give you a direction to go. We have heard that being informed is the first step to being prepared, and it's true. By being informed, we can always change direction, if required, based on the new information we acquire. We are the architect of our lives, build wisely. Go back to the draft board, and build in the present as an informed student.

"Those who never change their minds, never change anything"-Winston S. Churchill

RECONSTRUCTION PHASE

Instructions to Build

> *"Give instruction to a wise man, and he will be still wiser; Teach a just man and he will increase in learning" (Proverbs 9:9 NKJV).*

The above verse is a proverb, which is considered a short piece of advice. It does not have to be drawn out, just straight to the point. Looking back at Genesis 2, we see God spending time alone with Adam. This is where God prepares Adam, instructing him on how to live a life worthy of God's glory. Before the Fall, Adam was conscious of God and his humanity. The greatest tool that an apprentice builder could ever receive is having a master builder as a mentor. *Man Cave Under Construction* in its explanation of man deals in detail with our humanity. Even Jesus's life, in some cases, dealing with His humanity. In Matthew 13:55 (NKJV), Jesus is referred to as the "carpenter's son," and in Mark 6:3, He is referred to as a "carpenter." This could suggest He was an apprentice of His earthly father, and that "building a tower" was an analogy based on what He had learned and/or experienced, which later became a platform for building spiritual insight that leads to salvation. A builder builds based on what he knows and can imagine, but a master builder can teach others based on their vast knowledge, experience, and insight. This is what God does—help you grow into your potential. The greatest mistake a man can make is failing to heed wisdom, but one who welcomes a challenge and constructive criticism will go far. The grace of good counsel is that the person giving the counsel can see what you cannot. We may not want correction, but we need someone in our lives to make us uncomfortable so the world can see the best versions of us.

Build with Curiosity

Curiosity is the desire to know. The curiosity to create something drove inventors who were frustrated with the way things were to make a difference. Galileo Galilei was in a church in Italy and was bored. A minor Earth tremor set a hanging chandelier swaying. He compared the time of each arc to his pulse! Later, he tried different weights, different lengths, and other variables, and discovered that the time of each arc was constant. This led to the invention of the pendulum clock. His curiosity created a better life for himself and others. In an article entitled "Curiosity and Inventions," Arthur Daemmrich wrote, "Curiosity and inventiveness is not a proprietary domain; it should be supported in people regardless of gender, race, or ethnicity." Curiosity is not bad, but what you intend to gain from it can be. Be careful to examine your curiosity and ask the question, Will my pursuit of it glorify God or add value to the quality of life?

Obtaining the Right Crew

When we think of construction work, we don't often think in terms of relationships, the environment, or the soil, but all of these components are key. For example, a company may sponsor team-building events to build relationships within that organization. The more you collaborate with others, the more successful you become. When you don't work with others, failure means no one is there to pick up the slack. The same principles apply when building anything of value. Relationships must enable a free flow of communication so that people are not operating independently of each other in silos. There must be a consistency of thinking and purpose.

A person building alone can take a lifetime; however, building with the right help will drastically reduce that. You must surround yourself with people who have your best interests in mind and have the passion to help you build. We all need each other's help, so don't let pride hinder your progress. When and if you need help, ask for it, but make sure you do so from the right people.

Two people are better off than one, for they can help each other succeed. [10] *If one person falls, the other can reach out and help. But someone who falls alone is in real trouble.* [11] *Likewise, two people lying close together can keep each other warm. But how can one be warm alone?* [12] *A person standing alone can*

*be attacked and defeated, but two can stand
back-to-back and conquer. Three are even
better, for a triple-braided cord is not easily
broken. (Ecclesiastes 4:9-12 NLT)*

As examined throughout the book, *Man Cave* is a
pattern of thinking. The default for men can easily become
isolation—it's easy to retreat into our caves. We feel we need
to go into our caves and deal with our issues on our own
as Adam did after the Fall. At times, we all need someone
to give us a hand, a listening ear, encouragement, and even
corrections. During the rebuilding process, realize that you
are not alone. Find a group of men or believers with whom
you can find strength. We need others who can relate to our
experiences and help us through them. Many have already
been through and overcome what you are experiencing. If
your weakness is drinking or drugs, it is necessary to find a
group that can help you stay away from such habits because
isolation or being with others who indulge in the act will
certainly draw you back to those bad habits.

The Right Environment

*"For where two or three gather together as my
followers, I am there among them" (Matthew
18:20 NLT).*

Note, that we are not the original audience to which
this verse was spoken. However, once we believe the spirit
resides in us. This means people can gather who have the
spirit of Christ in them, and because he resides in you, he
is in the midst. This suggests you are like-minded when

it comes to Christ. Not only are the right people required to build a man, but the right environment is important too. Wisdom will give us insight into where to build. The Greek translation is "Gather together in my name." The environment to build is created when you associate with like-minded people, as it refers to Christ and His teachings. The Word of God and the presence of God set a standard that prevents you from being consumed by the drama that distorts your thinking.

It is important to surround yourself with people who follow Christ. They can support you in your attempt to build a life. Being in the presence of other believers will create a culture that represents your lifestyle. We must not forsake assembly with other believers. You need an environment that exemplifies your relationship with God and your expression of praise for Him. As men, we need to be reminded that the spirit of God lives in us. When Adam was in God's presence, he was supplied with all he needed. Life began to crumble when Adam became separated from God through his disobedience.

The Right Tools

> "Don't worry about anything; instead, pray about everything. Tell God what you need and thank him for all he has done. 7 Then you will experience God's peace, which exceeds anything we can understand. His peace will guard your hearts and minds as you live in Christ Jesus" (Philippians 4:6-7 NLT).

Without the right tools, your success will be limited. The more you remain in communication with God, the less you will be distracted by the tactics of the enemy. One of the most powerful tools you can carry from day today is prayer. Prayer is a dialogue between heaven and Earth, and as with any relationship, communication is key. In prayer, you must spend as much time listening as you spend talking. There is a time for all things, and wisdom will present time for listening and speaking.

> *"But without faith, it is impossible to please Him, for he who comes to God must believe that He is and that He is a rewarder of those who diligently seek Him." (Hebrews 11:6-7 NKJV)*

It is important to remember that believing the gospel of Christ leads to salvation. It is the premise of faith. Your actions in the rebuilding process are a response to what you have communicated to God, but also what you believe about Him. What you hear becomes the building blocks of how you live. As James 2:17 (AMP) states, "So too, faith if it does not have works [to back it up], is by itself dead [inoperative and ineffective]." The consistency of your communication indicates that the relationship is a close one and that you trust God at His Word. Faith is a result of believing what was communicated. This too validates your relationship with God.

Our reconstruction brings clarity to our purpose of reconnecting with our Father through the message of Christ. The message is of Him dying in our place to position us in the right relationship with the Father. This atonement reversed what originally separated man from Him. The Fall of man was the result of Adam's acceptance of an alternative message—they would be like God, knowing good and evil—that was presented by the serpent in the garden. This meant Adam and Eve rejected the original message that was already in them. The blueprint of man revealed possessed everything required to live a fulfilled life. Hence, the only thing that condemns us after Christ died a spiritual death in our place is the rejection of what God did through Christ for us. That is unbelief. Thus, you can't start building until you accept Christ as the cornerstone or foundation of the life you are building. The building has nothing to do with Salvation because Christ has done this work, however, we are responsible for growth in the knowledge of Him.

Adam was in a relationship with God before he was in a relationship with anyone or anything else. No one else existed, just him and God. Our way of building a relationship with God, however, begins with us seeking Him: "But seek first the kingdom of God and His righteousness, and all these things shall be added to you" (Matthew 6:33 NKJV). The word "seek" in Greek implies being constant and continual. So, although God intended for Adam to have relationships with a wife and his children, the relationship between Him and Adam was also meant to continue. As such, we are never to let other relationships deter us from our relationship with God as we live by the guidance of the Holy Spirit.

God's relationship with us involves teaching us how to build relationships with others. After all, man is to resemble

Him in character. The DNA of God is to be visible in man's qualities and lifestyles. We possess His DNA because we become sons through salvation. The DNA is His Spirit in us. I say this with the understanding of the use, in Colossians 1:8, of "firstborn" from the Greek word "prototokos." It means Christ is the prototype of what the church should resemble in its nature. We can hear God speak clearly when we yield singularly and uninterruptedly. This way, God is spiritually present and we are physically available. The greatest disconnect of any relationship—not just one with God—is to be physically present but mentally, emotionally, and spiritually absent. As men, we must remain connected to God and those close to us in all spectrums. I recalled hearing an observation that "before Eve was made, God spent time with Adam, and while Adam was asleep, God spent time with Eve." This indicates that all relationships should begin one-on-one with God, the one who made us. Spending time with God promotes spiritual maturity, but also natural understanding.

Where Do I Begin?

Father, we thank You for the leading of the Holy Spirit and guidance through the understanding of Your word. We pray that every decision we make is through careful examination of Your purpose. We pray that before career, marriage, or children, we make sure we are in a position to become successful through what we say, envision,

and incorporate the right timing and working
through the process. In Jesus' name, we pray.

Reconstruction should resemble God's original intent. There was a purpose of me covering influence earlier because whatever information you are influenced by will produce your reality, good, bad, or indifferent. It is important to deconstruct those things that are contrary to what you are intending to build. We were designed to build; however, your old thoughts can come in conflict with your identity if your mind is not renewed in the mirror of God's word. In Genesis chapter 1, God's purpose in the creation of man became our microcosm of what man's resemblance or likeness to God was supposed to look like. The image of God, or original intent of God, was designed to suit the environment he inhabited. God demonstrates four things in creation that should be exemplified in every believer for an effective earthly existence. These are essential elements identified from a simple examination of the text. They are his ability to speak, envision, understand timing, and work. It corresponds to a mandate for structural consistency, so he could possess the full capacity to build, primarily as it relates to his existence. We were built to do the same.

"And God said," is the first representation that echoes throughout chapter 1 of Genesis. The response to what God said is always, "It was so." What God says has credence and purpose. He does not say anything unless it is set out to accomplish that which is spoken. Likewise, what we say should be a representation of what we believe. There should be a life representation in our words. We have often heard the adage "Your word is your bond." What we say verifies that what we do is the same. Adam spoke, and every animal became what he called them. Man's purpose is to speak words of life into or over everything connected to him because doing so reflects a likeness to God. This means what you say should correspond to like action. What you say sets into motion every structure for the environment you're in. What you say is ultimately tied to how you think. How you think is an accumulation of what you have allowed to influence you.

Can we even conceptualize what it means for God to say, "Let us make man" (Genesis 1:26 KJV)? When we imagine making something, we are limited by our imaginations, but with God, there is no limit. God had to envision a detailed process of intent and functionality. It entailed insight and foresight. From the context of his responsibility, what Adam saw was what God showed him. He did not operate on what he was shown on his terms. The idea here is to always seek God to understand His plans for our lives. He knows far more about us than we know about ourselves. We must emulate these actions to have the best chance to narrate our success. This allows you to see your potential needs before they arise. We can't expect things to just manifest themselves, we must be the project manager who presents a blueprint of a well-thought-out plan.

The Importance of Timing

There is an elevator in a downtown Houston building that, after you reach a certain floor, requires you to get off and onto another elevator as a means to continue your journey up. Otherwise, if you remain on that elevator, it will go back down. The life lesson is in timing and the required movement, and what it means to everything connected to it.

With everything we do, proper timing is important—*Kairos*, God's timing is vital. In this timetable, God brings order to events because he has them all strategically planned out. Every moment is connected to the next. "And God made two great lights; the greater light to rule the day, and the lesser light to rule the night" (Genesis 1:16 KJV) before "The Lord God formed man of the dust of the ground" (Genesis 2:7 KJV). This is because, without light, man would walk in darkness and not be unable to complete his earthly assignment. The man was the last of his creations. This means the perquisites had already been provided. He had every required for a man to successfully inhabit the earth. We talked earlier about positioning for success because entering anything prematurely can create debt that you can't afford, children you are not prepared to raise, and marriages that you don't have adequate resources to sustain, which create burdens that can take a lifetime to recover from.

Uber's success is a product of timing. They utilize cell phone technology in two facets; it allows them to connect with anyone, anywhere with GPS capability. This allows both the rider and driver to interface with each other's location with the ability to communicate in the process. Note from the text that there was an outlined day that corresponds with everything God did. It is important to plan and put in place a time frame by which you plan to complete it. No time is a good time if there is no planned time to complete it.

We hear God speak in Genesis chapter 1, but then we see the activity of God at work in the process of creating man in Genesis 2:7 (KJV). "God formed man of the dust of the ground." God's making of a man introduces evidence of physical activity. Afterward, he mandates man to work in Genesis 2:14 (KJV). The work was to teach him how to manage and develop what was in his care. 'Work,' translated from Hebrew, also means 'to become.' God gave Adam a starting point. He had to work on what he had until it was cultivated into what it could *become* through the process of time. Like that of a seed, it is time for it to become the product. If you see the big picture, we are to become whom we are by realizing our realities in Christ. Our process is to be translated beyond where we start into everything connected to Him, which all require work. Note, that salvation takes believing, but growth and human sustainability take work. For us, the first thing man must do is work on himself, because man must learn to build in himself before he is allowed to build anything or anyone else. Work is a requirement when expecting results.

This begins with knowing that we are building an intimate relationship with the Father and that communication is required in humanity and fellowship with Him. This is to be done not sparingly but continuously. The reconstruction of man began at the cross. The first Adam delivered us into sin, but the second Adam, Jesus, came to deliver us from it. It starts with a change of heart— something Adam did not express after the Fall. Instead, he hid and blamed someone else for his actions. Help is granted when we accept Jesus taking our place on the cross to restore our relationship with the Father. We must take on a new way of thinking that separates us from the old process of living. The way the serpent presented the tree and the way Adam and Eve perceived it was the reason for the Fall. This illustrates why it is imperative to change how we think. The mind is part of our humanity, and we must guard it against this culture and all negative influences.

"And be not conformed to this world: but be ye transformed by the renewing of your mind, that ye may prove what is that good, and acceptable, and perfect, will of God" *(Romans 12:2 KJV).*

Today, prayer, worship, and the study of the Word are the avenues to a continuous, intimate relationship with God. Praying to God is how we can communicate with Him. It is an intimate fellowship that requires an invitation and response. God will not force Himself upon you. His desire is for you to seek Him, which you must do wholeheartedly. As with any intimate relationship, we must look forward to and desire to meet Him in fellowship, the study of the word, and prayer.

When God created the first man, he was naked and unashamed. Today, we think it is unmanly to be men of God as if it makes us less of a man. However, our strength is embedded in our worship because our dependence is solely on God. Worship is simply showing adoration and reverence to Him. There are two powerful reasons to worship Him: first he loves us so much that He gave His only begotten Son to save us from eternal death and second, we are now the Sons of God and are adopted into the Royal Family.

He is our direction. Psalm 119:105 (NKJV) writes, "Your word is a lamp to my feet, And a light to my path." This means that the Word gives light to the direction I am required to walk. Through daily study, God illuminates our thinking. Living in a world that is influenced by the constructs of ungodly living, we require instruction that helps us to combat those tactics. Our journey is that of faith, which comes through hearing God's Word. The Word generates hope, comfort, and direction.

What Is My Name (Identity)?

"I will make you a great nation; I will bless you And make your name great, And you shall be a blessing" (Genesis 12:2-3 NKJV).

When God spoke to Abraham, He promised him a great nation and to make his name great for his obedience. Abraham believed the promise, and it was counted unto him as righteousness (Genesis 15:6 KJV). We have an even greater promise. What makes our name GREAT is based on what Christ did on the cross to rebuild our relationship with the Father. Like Abraham did with his promise, we must believe. The actions of Christ took led us to righteousness and believing that message makes us sons. Walking in Christ's example brings us into the reality of the Father's plans for us. In this, our names are revealed because we are the reflection through our demonstration of service to others as the new creation in Christ.

With this, we also have the responsibility to represent

His great name in our humanity, because we are a representation of him on the earth. It is what we do and how we represent ourselves that helps others to know our new name, the name of Christ. What do others think of your name? Regardless of the answer, your name represents something to someone, whether you desire it to or not. When someone hears your name, do they think of a liar or cheater? Do children cringe in fear when your name is mentioned? Furthermore, what does your name mean to you? You will forever be known by the identity you create. Your reputation and representation will precede you. The blueprint of your identity is determined by your activity.

Your name must present in your character a commitment that is consistent and transferable. This means others must be able to carry what the name represents far after you are gone. Your goal should be to continue improving. Life is about learning and improving on what already exists. Doing so reveals your greatness, which comes from God, the Father when He calls you. God said to Abraham, "I will make your name great" (Genesis 12:2 NIV). He will make our names great because we are His and He is great! We are His sons. Greatness is not measured by worldly standards, but it comes when you know who you are, and the evidence follows you. Although, we are both limited and fallible, having a great name and representing Him in our lives means our greatness transcends our mistakes.

In addition, He makes our names great by building us from the inside out and the bottom up, foundationally. We build based on what is seen, but He builds based on the elements of faith, which are unseen. The fundamental building block is trusting God. In addition, we allow the

Holy Spirit to lead in the building process. When we build, we serve. Time is the greatest element in humanity. It must be managed wisely because it will eventually end for us in this realm. Build others as you build yourself so that others will also possess the ability to build. This will ultimately make your name great because you are in Christ. What made Abraham's name great was that he so strongly believed in God regardless of circumstances. We must tear down what we have already built so His will may prevail and build us anew. This construction is not for nothing. It is necessary so that we may carry His name, His likeness, and fulfill His purpose.

Short story, in summary, I decided to start an upholstery business for secondary income. I remembered a Fabric Supplier whereby my father would buy supplies for his upholstery shop. I decided to go in and open an account. During the application process, I mentioned my dad use to come here all the time when he was alive, so he asked who my father was. I told him, and immediately the gentlemen lit up and teared up at the same time. He said, I surely missed your father, because he was a good man. He excitedly processed my application while telling me stories of my dad bringing everyone in their office sweet potatoes sometimes when he drove in from Louisiana. This business is in Houston, TX where I reside. Here is the moral of the story. My Father's name allowed me to bypass the red tape and I was welcomed into an extended relationship with people I never knew. This man went out of his way to get me books of fabric when there was a shortage and in demand. This was not the result of anything I had done, but it was because of my father's name. Doesn't this remind you of our Heavenly Father? A good name is to be chosen rather than great riches" Proverbs 22:1a (NKJV).

How Do I Come Out of Hiding?

In this book, the idea of the "mancave" represents a pattern of thinking that we have been subjected to, and one of the results manufactured from this form of thinking could be hiding. It appears that hiding is a result of the fall of Adam. The shame of insufficiencies and falling below our worth reproduces this behavior over and over. Hiding in this instance is escaping as a way of dealing with the issue. The enemy often uses shame and inadequacy to drive men into hiding. Both the spiritual and natural perspectives are relevant because our inadequacies can lead to hiding in both. Although scars remain from the sins of your past, God has redeemed you through the price Jesus paid on the cross. Falling is not the opportunity to isolate yourself but amid scrutiny the strength to get back up.

"Whom his own self bares our sins in His own body on the tree..." (1 Peter 2:24 KJV)

"There is therefore now no condemnation to them which are in Christ." (Romans 8:1 KJV). The enemy's tactic is to make you question the validity of God's Word like he did with Adam and Eve, but through perfect knowledge of Jesus, that reality is clear. You don't have to hide from what God delivered you. It is your past, not the future or present.

Isaiah gives a good illustration of what that looks like: "I, *even* I am He who blots out your transgressions for My own sake, And I will not remember your sins" (Isaiah 43:25

NKJV). Use your obstacles in life as evidence, because the enemy cannot expose what you have already revealed. The transparency you present will become relevant for the transformation of others. Our lives are on display so that the world can find hope through our victories.

Once we understand the identity of our spiritual reality, we realize it is eternal. This indicates that we don't have to hide, and our physical reality should exemplify the same. The difference between the two is what Christ has done, and what we must do. As men, we often hold to a certain construct of manhood: "Don't show your weakness." This in turn causes us to go into hiding so that our uncertainties are not revealed as we attempt to solve them on our own. What we have learned is that failure and inadequacies are a part of the human experience. We are to manage what we have control over without hiding, and not be afraid to say "I need help" when we don't have the answers.

How Do I Become a Good Steward Over My Health?

Earlier, I asked a series of questions about "Where we are..." with self-reflection in mind. I wanted everyone to think about it, so I reiterated it, so we don't lose sight of intentional change. We don't have to hope for change, we are change agents. Our relationship to the Father through Christ confirms our identity. It is tailored to teach us stewardship and service. It starts with taking care of ourselves.

*"Beloved, I pray that in every way you may succeed and prosper and **be in good health***

[physically], just as [I know] your soul prospers [spiritually]" (III John 2 AMP).

We are in three parts, Spirit, Soul (mind), and body. It is important to look at this verse in reverse. The essence of man is spirit but encapsulated in the physical body. The soul or mind is the communication center between both. The body is necessary for the spirit to bring activity to the earth. The section of this text requires that we don't take our physical health for granted, even as a grow mentally and spiritually, because it is necessary for our continued life on Earth. We are to be stewards of our spirits, minds, and bodies. What we expose our body to physically and our minds to mentally will determine our success and the consequences of our actions. It is impossible to inhabit the Earth without possessing a healthy body to do so. Being aware of the potential hazards and making wise decisions can both improve and preserve your quality of life. The value of our humanity exceeds our titles or occupations, because the moment health is lost, everything associated with it is also lost.

Over time, what we put into our bodies will have either a positive or negative effect. For example, I have had high levels of low-density lipoproteins (LDL), and my cardiologist told me to avoid red meat and exercise regularly. In my case, exercising or avoiding red meat independently is a good thing, but the right thing is to do them collectively. It is like saying, "I provide for my family but sometimes I cheat on my wife." The difference between good and right could mean completing the equation by doing exactly what is required. It is good that you provide for your family.

It is wrong to cheat. It is right to be a good provider and husband.

The Bible indicates that exercise has a purpose: *"For physical training is of some value"* (1 Timothy 4:8 NIV). The entire text does not minimize or negate the full essence of it, but in comparison, godliness is of greater value, because it is for the present life, and the life to come.

According to Harvard Health Publishing (Harvard Medical School), "you can increase your chances of having a healthy heart with regular physical activity, which raises healthy HDL cholesterol levels and reduces unhealthy LDL cholesterol and triglycerides. It also lowers blood pressure, burns body fat, and lowers blood sugar levels, all of which benefit heart health. The power of exercise to help the heart cannot be understated."

I struggled with high cholesterol for years, and my doctor prescribed medications to help me. But I chose to reduce my cholesterol the natural way. After 30 minutes of daily exercise for 1 month, 4 days a week, and changing my diet, my total cholesterol decreased from 239 to 205, and my LDL went down from 187 to 151. It has significantly changed how I feel physically. Just like my walk with Christ, I realized it must be a lifestyle because it cannot only affect your life but also your quality of life. Quality of life is life.

Harvard Health Publishing also indicates that there are other benefits, such as keeping your brain sharp, controlling blood sugar levels, possibly lowering the risk of underlying health conditions, and helping you stay strong and mobile. My grandfather lived to be 99 years old. He stayed active, working in the garden or chopping wood. That was his exercise. There are also bonuses. According to an article published on Health.com entitled "How Exercise Can Improve Your Sex Life":

In men, regular exercise appears to be a natural Viagra. It's associated with a lower risk of erectile problems. In one study, sedentary middle-aged men assigned to participate in a vigorous exercise program for nine months reported more frequent sexual activity, improved sexual function, and greater satisfaction. Those whose fitness levels increased most saw the biggest improvements in their sex lives. (Davis, 2017)

To live hazardously as if there is no tomorrow means you have lost consciousness of today. By this, I am referencing living a life of physical danger. Perhaps you have heard the saying, "You are so spiritually minded until you are no earthly good." I have learned to understand, according to my walk, what it could entail. Sometimes, we expect God to do what God expects us to do. We should always pray for answers, but we also need to take care of our bodies and even take prescribed medication until our healing is present. This also includes getting proper rest, reducing stress, and eliminating drugs and alcohol that lead to the decline of your health. The miracle is to believe in God for healing and stop doing those things that caused it in the first place.

Consider eating foods that lower your blood pressure, cholesterol, and chances of heart attacks and strokes. Exercise daily, because staying active is important. Be knowledgeable of what is going on inside your body so you can preserve your health. According to the American Heart Association,

Regular physical activity can relieve stress, anxiety, depression, and anger. Do you know that 'feel good sensation' you get after doing something physical? Think of it as a happy pill with no side effects! Most people notice they feel better over time as physical activity becomes a regular part of their lives. (Retrieved from https://www.heart.org/en/healthy-livng)

What Should Be the Proper Perspective Regarding Sex?

Today, there is a lot of sexual content on social media to contend with it. This content can become influential in our thinking. It creates an invitation to the eye gate and lures you down a showroom of sexual desires. It presents to you every shape cover and seduction tactic to make it desirable to you. Guarding your mind against such things is necessary to keep you from being consumed.

Two things to consider in managing these desires are discipline and cause. Why discipline and cause? Discipline and causes work alongside each other. If there is no cause, there is nothing to force you to become disciplined. There must be a drive or a motivation. Paul once said in Corinth, "I discipline my body and bring it into subjection" (1 Corinthians 9:24-17 NKJV). He was speaking to those who were familiar with the Isthmian Games, in which the competitors trained for a race (the cause). They changed their diets and behaviors and trained so they could compete at a higher level. The competitors exercised discipline to go beyond their natural, untrained stage, so they could be successful in the cause.

Sex may be a need, but we ought to discipline ourselves to foster our relationship with Christ—the first cause. That is fleeing fornication. When we are single, we do it so that we may not sin against God, but please Him. The second cause is being faithful in marriage, so we do not sin against our spouse. In principle, what we learn before marriage and just carried over into marriage. Man's desire should be for his wife, and not for any other influences or selfish sexual gratification.

How do you manage sexual desire the natural way? We must die to ourselves and our fleshy desires daily. The path to success is similar to a strict diet. We must guard ourselves against the strategic weapons of the enemy. We must be careful about what we entertain. When we watch sexually explicit movies or visit strip clubs, our desire for fantasy creates an appetite for sin and is sustained every time we return to it. We tend to have open minds to the things that are hard to forget. You can't unsee what you see. We may find it difficult to block out what we have seen. If there is no memory of it, then there is no temptation. By feeding on the Word of God and not objectifying a woman's body, we guard ourselves against such things occurring.

How Do I Understand a Need for Emotions?

"Jesus wept" (John 11:35 NKJV). We can probably give two good reasons why we think Jesus wept. We see one through the eyes of the Jews who exclaimed, "See how he loved him" as a response to why Jesus wept. It was viewed as a response to the loss of someone you love. This would be a good explanation to the onlooker. Humanly, the death of Lazarus and the relationship he shared warranted tears, but spiritually, death is the result of Adam's sin, which Christ would ultimately have to pay for our redemption. More so, death is the last enemy that Jesus himself would eventually defeat. This verse, the shortest in the Bible, is one of Jesus' most powerful human expressions.

Because it is taboo for men to cry, men cry in a space where they can trust their tears to fall and not be rendered as weakness. Consequently, it is most often when he is alone. He feels it breaches everyone who looks to him for strength. An article in Global News by Dani-Elle Debe on Feb 22, 2018, states "Despite what men may think or what "Social norms" may still exist, women actually do prefer a man who isn't afraid to wear his emotions on his sleeve, a new survey has found. According to a survey of 1500 people by Elite Singles, 95 percent of women say they prefer a man who is open about his emotions, while 97 percent say they find that men crying is considered strong, natural, or healthy. "Women long to have an emotional connection with their significant others, and this is discovered when men are transparent in their emotions.

Contrary to the claims that real men don't cry, crying is how God designed the body to heal itself physically and emotionally. Where we were told not to cry, we are essentially taught not to heal. There was no way to unpack what we felt, so we suppress it. Whether you prefer to cry publicly or privately, it is a healthy release. After the death of Kobe Bryant, fans and men who knew him wept openly. It is an outward expression of inward emotion. Research has found that in addition to being self-soothing, crying releases oxytocin and endorphins. These chemicals make people feel good and may also ease both physical and emotional pain. In this way, crying can help reduce pain and promote a sense of well-being.

I fought with every fiber of my being to hold back the tears at my father's funeral. I allowed the view of manhood to prevent me from expressing how I felt about my dad. Men often wear dark shades at funerals to hide the pain revealed in their eyes. As boys, many of us were told that we aren't supposed to cry, but Jesus's tears in the case of Lazarus builds a different narrative. It was the same relationship I had with my father. I loved him for who he was and for the time we shared. His passing left with me a range of emotions. However, Ecclesiastes 3:4 (KJV) reminds us that there is a time for everything: "A time to laugh … a time to cry." But we find many men thinking it is unmanly to do so.

I have also wept, privately, after failing or seeing my deficiencies. Even though I sometimes feel as though I have not done everything to acquire victory, sometimes some of the greatest victories come through the lessons of defeat. I think of the line from *The Samaritan*, "If you keep on doing what you have always done, then you keep on being what you have always been. Nothing changes unless you make it change." The only way you see life is to seek to understand everything that surrounds it, then adapt and grow. A different dimension of manhood needs to be known, so we can promote understanding of self and become *effective* in relationships with our counterpart who processes information differently.

This other dimension is called emotional intelligence, which is defined as the capacity to be aware of, control, and express one's emotions, and to handle interpersonal relationships judiciously and sympathetically. Mental intelligence does not equate to emotional intelligence. Contrary to the popular belief, having an emotion does not make us weak. Rather, it reveals our strength. When we suppress our emotions, we are simply hiding from ourselves and masking our fears. Unlike some women, who are more emotionally in touch with how they feel, men feel emotions but rarely deal with them, so we never heal. Since we often hide our emotions, it makes it more difficult for us to relate to others on an emotional level. Emotionally, men are often compressed, which causes us to require a release of our frustrations all at once, which can be an issue when relating to ourselves and others.

The value and benefit of such emotional maturity are demonstrated in the scripture, "Whoever is slow to anger is better than the mighty, and he who rules his spirit than he who takes a city" (Proverbs 16:32 ESV). The first step is to sensibly evaluate those emotions within us. Second, absorb and relate to the emotions of others. The two are conduits to each other. You don't have to be emotional to show emotions, nor do you need to allow them to control you, but you must learn to understand them to manage them in light of the relationships you will encounter. This means learning how to communicate how we feel. Historically, incidents in our youth left us feeling awkward and like an outcast without an outlet to communicate our fears and anxieties, so we dared not talk about how we felt. Being a man does not equate to the absence of emotions. Instead, it's about governing the response and how they are released. We often shut down emotionally to prevent ourselves from succumbing to feelings that we think make us appear weak. This thinking, however, is the result of problematic cultural views. The key is to determine or establish under what circumstance or environment you are comfortable expressing yourself in this manner. In relationships, it is necessary to empathize with those requiring you to feel or rather relate to how they feel. Not only will you be required to be emotionally available, but most of all emotionally engaged.

Oftentimes, a man wants to be emotionally accessible but lacks a model for how to do that. Many of us have learned to release our emotions through sports, but not through conversations. I believe it is a sign of strength when we can manage how we release our emotions and communicate frustration creatively and intelligently.

How Do I Become a Financial Steward?

"A feast is made for laughter, And wine makes merry; But money answers everything" (Ecclesiastes 10:19 NKJV).

The statement in the above quotation that "money answers everything" is relative to money being the answer to those things for which money is required—unfortunately, even in things such as bribery and extortion. Relative to the nature of humanity, money is the currency required for occupancy on the Earth. Food and shelter require money.

Neither businesses nor churches can function without it, because everything has an operating expense. Homes going into foreclosure and cars being repossessed, both of which can drive a relationship to fail, have one common denominator: the lack or mismanagement of money.

Money is important because it is a resource required to buy and sell necessities on Earth. As men, our desire for money should relate to taking care of ourselves and our families and the furthering of the gospel, even if it requires a greater sacrifice on our behalf. Remember, you don't have to be Superman, just be super wise.

Here is a thought to ponder in the man cave. We may be familiar with the adage "We don't plan to fail; we just fail to plan." Use any simple saving calculator to calculate your future. Take the opportunity to invest in yourself.

Like any construction project, the moment you cut corners is the moment a countdown begins to when that cut corner will expose itself. The same attitude applies to anything in life. If you do life by half-measures, some things will require a do-over at a cost you will not be prepared to pay. There is a fine line between "Can I afford to?" and "Can I afford not to?" The simple determination can be whether you are looking at the short term or the long term. You can choose to live in the moment, but when you desire to retire, you can't afford to stop working. Take retirement planning, for example. If you look at the short term, you might say that you have time, but if you look long term, you envision small investments over a long period. Building principles are important, but you can't build without a blueprint.

Building Wealth

"Take possession of the land and settle in it, for I have given you the land to possess" (Numbers 33:53 NIV).

This scripture was talking to specific people at a specific time, referencing a specific promise. It was not talking to us. Today, we all may or may not want to possess something that we consider wealth. The way we settle and possess is different. Whatever form such differences take, this verse still has relevance, especially if we talk about power and wealth. Possessing land is a symbol of wealth in most cultures, but we often consider money a type of wealth. In any instance, it takes effort to acquire anything in life. Work is a mandate to position you and your family for success. The word of God says "But if any provide not for his own, and especially for those of his own house, he hath denied the faith, and is worse than an infidel" 1 Timothy 5:8 (KJV).

I will approach this point from their experience; however, we also see this promise as a pointer to things to come as related to Salvation because Abraham believed God according to Hebrews 11. We often hear statements like "Those of the world are prospering and believers are not." The truth is, we all operate under the same law on Earth, whether you are a believer or not. For the most part, we have to work and pay bills. Matthew 5:45 (NKJV) states, "for He makes His sun rise on the evil and on the good and sends rain on the just and on the unjust." Both the just and unjust farmer need to know the proper seeding time when it comes to planting a crop. Therefore, so long as the conditions and the techniques are the same, the harvest of a believer and a nonbeliever should be the same. Our success on Earth is connected to the effort we give to the area in which we intend to succeed. The results rest solely in man's ability to cultivate what he has been entrusted with, and God entrusted Adam with being a steward of the Earth. Seeds are for the future, not the present, and any seed that is not used will be wasted. You need to do something every day to bring that seed to harvest. The seed is your construction project. God will not do this for you.

When it comes to careers, the principles of sowing and reaping still apply. The capacity to pursue a dream is available to anyone, but achieving that dream requires taking advantage of opportunities. Look at your seed and envision what it could produce. You will be rewarded by the seed when you harvest it, but it must be cultivated, otherwise, it becomes a wasted seed. Going to medical school and not completing it will not produce the wealth capacity of a doctor. Nurture your seed, be it a creative thought, inventions, books, athletics, entertainment, or any other career, and receive the result of that you've sown.

God has given you the strength and energy to obtain the wealth needed to live your life. But you must exercise this power. Let's get a view of what that looks like. No matter the career path you take—whether to college, military, trade school, or your own business—it takes energy and perseverance to reach the end of that path. Long nights and frustrating days are common to all these journeys but shall obtain or produce their results. I learned a trade of upholstery from my dad, which I used to make extra money alongside my primary occupation. One may argue that this side of occupation chose me, but in all fairness, I chose to accept, learn, and utilize it.

God creates environments for the right relationships to be developed to help you gain employment and opportunity. These relationships help to connect you with others and resources. We have often heard the saying, "It is not always what you know, but whom you know." It is our responsibility to nurture relationships that help expose us to other opportunities. This is in addition to seeking our passions and understanding our gifts and talents because these are things that give us the chance to accomplish our desires. You need to do something every day to eradicate fear and distractions to bring those abilities to manifestation. The question is, are you maximizing your potential or just settling for enough to get by? You must foster your relationships and abilities so you can provide as you should.

The reality is, that wealth means something different to different people. In some cases, many choose their passions over gaining more possessions, because that is where their treasure lies. You are only as successful as the time, talent, and treasure you invest. In addition, you are only as successful as you are prepared. Many families work all their lives and have nothing at the age of retirement. When we are young and energetic, it can be hard to imagine what life is like in old age, but that time comes quicker than expected. Planning for retirement early provides security in times of uncertainty. COVID-19 revealed that most people do not have the economic capacity to go six months without pay. Learning early to create wealth through merely saving is important. It may not gain and it certainly doesn't lose. You get exactly what you put in. Under the right investment strategy, your money has the potential to work for you. Establishing 401k and other investment strategies is critical for long-term survival. To be something extra, you need to do something extra. At times, that extra can be planting a seed that can be harvested for your future and future generations. Your faith sets things into motion, but intentional efforts bring them to pass.

Here is a thought. At the age of 20, a $2,000 investment and $150.00 a month commitment into a mutual fund that has averaged just 6% yearly could net you $389,008.84 over 40 years. This may be outside other investments. Some mutual funds have shown growth of over 10%. This is not typical, and you must do your homework if you do not have an advisor. For a shorter term, you may elect a bigger investment and commitment. The money you waste could be the money you gain if used wisely. Use any simple savings calculator to calculate your future. Take the opportunity to invest in yourself. Results may vary, so please consult a professional financial advisor when making such decisions.

The task of *Man Cave Under Construction* is to exhaustively explore as many aspects of manhood as possible, especially the ones we often overlook until it is too late. It is important to look ahead as a visionary and plan wisely. I often look back at what I could have done differently. Those things would have positioned me for greater success. I can't change my past, but I can impact my future.

Another one of these is wealth management, whereby a portfolio is designed for retirement and is also a backup for your family if something were to happen to you. It is important to plan out beneficiaries, so there is no confusion or turmoil among the family. So, before the wife, children, and everything that follows, make sure you position yourself to manage an effective and efficient life. *Man Cave* the book is intended to inform you to think about all things, but it is your responsibility to carry these out.

Leave a legacy, not debt. Some of your debt doesn't die with you. As Michael Aloi notes, "Some types of debts are forgiven when you die, and others could haunt your family until they're paid off." Coupled with the burden of your death, they now face the additional burden of your debt. Social media is flooded with GoFundMe accounts that attempt to help families in some of their toughest moments. If some plans were enacted before those unforeseeable events, how much peace would you feel, knowing that your family will be ok?

We have no idea what will happen or when it will occur, but it is always good to know you are prepared. We often wait until we are older to invest in insurance policies, associating death with age, when coverage becomes unaffordable. It is also good to have a policy with your job, and one independent of your job, because if you lose your job, buying a policy is the last thing that will cross your mind.

Proverbs 13:22 (NKJV) "A good man leaves an inheritance to his children's children"—can stand alone in scripture. In this instance, the pretext and post-text may be different. The idea here is that you must have something to give something. In other words, you can't give what you don't possess. It is about positioning yourself to be in a place to give or leave something. It could be in the event you are alive or dead. One of the most valuable things to pass down is the gospel of Christ because it is eternal in nature. You can leave a business that you are retiring from that is designed to be handed down, or an insurance policy after you are gone. It could be a college fund he or she possesses as they enter college. It doesn't have to be money but could be giving them life tools to build from, or even teaching them a trade. College is expensive, so planning for your children's education is mandatory. One thing to consider early on is your children's education and future. We always hope that our children receive scholarships to help pay for higher education, but such rewards are not guaranteed. My son graduated high school with a 4.0, summa cum laude, and a score of 31 on his ACT. Nonetheless, he was not awarded an academic scholarship. It is a good idea to set up an educational fund when your children are young because preparing for this early will reduce the burden later. It is our responsibility to provide for their success even if the system we depend on does not. It would be a disservice to our children's futures if they were to find themselves in financial ruin before their adult lives had even begun.

Building and Restoring Relationships

I Am My Brother's Keeper

> *"Then the LORD said to Cain, 'Where is Abel your brother?' He said, 'I do not know. Am I my brother's keeper?'" (Genesis 4:9 NKJV)*

One of the most powerful moments of my ministry took place several years back. It is not that I had never experienced a powerful move of God, but this was different because it involved men. I was teaching a co-ed Bible study when a friend, who later became one of my best friends, said, "Let's start an all-men Bible study." This was supposed to be a place where we could talk about male challenges. When the new Bible study group began, I had no idea what was to come. Men who at first glance seemed confident and secure found a safe place among brothers to become transparent about what weighed on their souls. They released feelings they had carried for years: infidelity, abuse, fears, and other types of brokenness we encounter as men but dare not talk about. It was in those moments that I saw men become free. From that experience, I learned that men often internalize their struggles but have no space to be authentic and work through them. Physically, men are drawn to a man cave (a place of solitude), the place where they can be authentic.

When God addressed Cain, God was not unaware of where Abel was or what had happened to him. It was a rhetorical question, and He asked Cain to make a point, not to get an answer. Cain's anger severed his relationship with his brother, and how he should have felt was hardened by his selfishness. We take from this text that having kinship doesn't necessarily mean there is a relationship. This ties back to the emotional emphasis of this book. Cain was unable to unpack the emotions that led to his actions. If we are not careful, our inability to resolve differences can lead to selfishness and the inability to empathize with others. Men need other men to hold them accountable, in a relationship like that of a brotherhood. Men need to draw strength from each other. Men don't need 'yes men,' but men who are strong enough to be truthful, spiritual enough to restore, and human enough to relate.

As men, we should consider the cost of brotherhood.

Have we been our brother's keeper? Let's be clear on what that looks like. Every man is responsible for keeping others from demonstrating behavior that becomes detrimental to them. A keeper has his brother's back, meaning even protecting him from himself. This does not mean helping him cover his sins but helping him take ownership of his actions and orchestrating a plan to overcome them. Manhood is about holding each other accountable and encouraging the opportunity for growth. We may view life from different perspectives but understanding each other's dilemmas and commonalities gracefully can help us understand how to help each other through life's battles. Indeed, this is precisely what the gospel exhorts us to do: "Therefore encourage one another and build each other up, just as in fact you are doing" (1 Thessalonians 5:11NIV).

Some brotherly relationships are developed through biological families, while others are formed through shared purpose. At times, the ones formed by way of shared purpose have a deeper connection because the brothers have experienced and walked through some of the same trials, but also have shared a common faith. In this, you are in the presence of someone with whom you are comfortable enough to be transparent. The scripture says, "Confess your faults one to another, and pray one for another, that ye may be healed" (James 5:16 KJV). This scripture could have applications for men in multiple areas, but for men who hide their feelings, pain, and expressions, it becomes a license to release what is normally internalized. In addition, to settling disputes among themselves.

The intent of healing, restoration, and instruction provides a platform for men to be honest and authentic with each other. After starting the Bible study, I mentioned earlier, exclusively for men, I was surprised by how men became more vocal and open. One of the men in the group became one of my best friends and at our jobs, we would talk and pray daily to gain strength from each other. We became accountability partners. Both of us were divorced, had kids, and were wrestling with sexual desires. I remember a conversation we had while working out. We talked about the women we were dating and inevitably talked about sex. We discussed not having sex with them until we are married since their bodies did not belong to us yet. These conversations kept us from jumping too quickly into gratifying our flesh. I was determined to please God but needed God's grace when I made mistakes, and I needed my friend to help me stay on the path. We become healed when we stop hiding from our insecurities and allow ourselves to depend on others. Others, in turn, depend on us to walk through our trials in Christ.

The greatest enemy to brotherhood is the feeling of shame and disgrace because it causes us to withdraw and prevents us from showing our true feelings. Whether it is about financial failure or general life failures, being able to be authentic can become the building block to other important relationships. Also detrimental to brotherhood is associating with those who do not see you as a brother as well: "He that walketh with wise men shall be wise: but a companion of fools shall be destroyed" (Proverbs 13:20 KJV). Remember we are brothers in Christ, but you cannot teach others until you have learned yourself.

CONCLUSION

"Then the LORD God planted a garden in Eden in the east, and there he placed the man he had made. ¹⁵ The LORD God placed the man in the Garden of Eden to tend and watch over it" (Genesis 2:8,15a NLT).

God is the architect and master builder, and we are His new creation, created in Christ. When God made man, He was designed to fulfill a purpose. He was created to occupy a space and time to which he is bringing glory to the Father. The man was to build with all that God entrusted him with. Like Adam, you have been given access to abilities that represents your gifts, creativity, ministries, and families. If you reject the tools and do not cultivate with them, they will wither in that place and will not produce what was intended. When they are neglected, all hope dies. Dreams die. Communities and cultures die. It becomes even more apparent when the man dies having not met his full potential.

Consider what it will cost to become a better man, a better husband, and a better father. At times, things happen beyond our control; however, many of the circumstances that surround us are related to mismanaging control over the things we have control over. This means failing to count the cost of the things we involve ourselves in. We make kids that we have no means or intent on raising, we make purchases we can't afford, and place ourselves in situations of physical danger. Cost is not always in what you pay, but in what you sacrifice. Your influence will either provide oxygen or suffocate those around you. When God made man, He made your seed such that it could reproduce life after itself. Therefore, be intentional. Everything you do must be done with a purpose in mind. Speak and live life intentionally. Every day will add new opportunities to build, but you must be willing to do so in wisdom.

Rome was not built in a day, and neither will those things that impact you. But if you consistently build in every area of your life, such as your faith, health, finances, and relationships—everything you need—over time you will see what you have intentionally built. Embrace your wife daily, look her in the eyes, and tell her you can't live life without her. Intentionally tell your kids that they are great so they will walk in greatness.

Man Cave is supposed to be a place of refuge. A place to retreat from the hustle and bustle of everyday life. It entails enjoying sports, listening to music, or whatever it takes to decompress from the anxieties and pressures of life. However, the greatest man cave is centered around how we think. It is what we have learned over the span of our life and how we process it within the confines of those things connected to us. In this place, if looking beyond the norm, you will find you have neglected what is most important due to antiquated principles. These principles unfortunately have built our realities. The main focus of

Man Cave Under Construction is to analyze and if needed, deconstruct those things we were taught to think about and reconstruct them into what we ought to think. Finally, the decision to live intentionally as a purposeful builder is left in the toolbox of choice for all men. Every day, be intentional and intentionally do something that will enhance your growth.

EXCERPT: THE OTHER SIDE OF YOU

"Many marriages would be better if the husband and the wife clearly understood that they are on the same side" -Zig Ziglar

The act of imprecating a phrase such as "I am leaving" in a midst of a marital disagreement can have a lasting effect. In her analytics, she is forever waiting on that day that you will leave for good. From that moment she became insecure. Although you may have meant "to get away in that moment" that is not what she heard. Your words can be both the blueprint and structure, so for your words to be carefully crafted your thinking must be transformed first. Even a disparity should be communicated in a way that assures her that you are on the same side.

We know influence plays a powerful role in how marriage is viewed. Each person will play out the version they have been exposed to. This is what they either witnessed growing up or expectations gathered from a social media guru, or even song lyrics. It doesn't matter if their version is fictitious or realistic. No one can expect what they are not willing to give. In many cases, perceptions are a carryover of what existed in their courting process. If they mistreated each other, it will carry over into marriage. If they managed their relationship in chaos, cursing, and insults, that is their norm. They will only see that as a norm, and seemingly healthy relationships will be viewed as abnormal. Hopefully, at this point, you value yourself enough to avoid relationships that will compromise your full potential, like drama, or those who seek after what you possess and not you.

The human relationship is one of God's most vital creations. His creative design was meant, in essence, to bring about fullness. It is one of the many ways God communicates with us in human form. The way we treat others, and ourselves, should display the very heart of our Father. Males and females are the same because both possess the ability to build love relationships, although they may differ in how they express themselves in them, and to what extent. We all, at some point, have experienced feelings of love, but not everyone has been loved based on their requirements or understood how to truly love someone the way God intended. Effectively loving someone means loving them down to their soul, beyond their faults and failures. To truly love, we must examine God's original intent for man and woman. Truly loving someone is not just a mere reflection of you, but a reflection of God, the One who first loved you.

This book continues from the same construct of positioning. A pivotal scripture that points to God's intentional nature of the husband is Genesis 2:21 (NIV): "So the Lord caused the man to fall into a deep sleep; and while he was sleeping, he took one of man's ribs and then closed up the place with flesh." The thought of interest I want to point out was that it was sacrificial. The man had to give up something. If you follow the thought pattern of the writer, you will see hidden in this passage of scripture a type of Christ, a type of John 3:16 moment. It was as if Moses was using a creative way of using the events in creation to teach salvation. The giving provided by God through a man always produces something purposeful from it—in both cases, a bride. Out of the sacrifice of Adam, Eve, a bride; out of the sacrifice of Christ, the Church, a bride. Paul's words in Ephesians 5:25 (KJV) exemplify this point. This passage seems to be a bridge between Moses's mode of communication and Paul's explanation, which is ultimately a pointer to Christ, an identification unifier. He said, "Husbands, love your wives, even as Christ also loved the church, and gave himself for it." This draws the similarity that the intentional nature of the husband toward his wife should be sacrificial. The marital design was to resemble Christ and the church, which is an inseparable union. This can be confirmed in Matthew 19:8 (KJV), which is a response to v.7: "He said to them, Moses because of the hardness of your hearts suffered you to put away your wives, but from the beginning, it was not so." Jesus' term "The beginning" here is a reference to Genesis. The only human separation was death, which is mentioned in Paul's writing in 1 Corinthians 7:39 (KJV). A commonality exists that prevents reconciliation in both human marriage and salvation is the hardness of hearts. So, if you reread Genesis 2:18 "Not good for man to be alone", it is really not good for man to be without Him or His presence. If you trust a person for happiness, you will find that is not possible.

I now will back up and point out a critical statement used

be present. Therefore, it is very important to learn about the person you plan to marry. I mean learn about her and not group her or associate with all women. Examine her uniqueness. My wife and I were platonic friends and had no interest in dating each other when we met five years before our marriage, but we would confide in each other, and seek each other advice about relationships and expectations. From this, we gained invaluable information about each other, which allowed us to make an informed decision about our compatibility.

Just because she is a good woman, it doesn't necessarily mean she is a good fit for you. Learning is an asset and ignorance is a liability. Immaturity will cause you to marry for the wrong reason. One of the prerequisites is learning, then knowing what the other person wants and needs. Then assess whether you can provide it or even know how to meet those expectations. Whenever there is an expectation, there is also disappointment when it can't be met.

There is the wisdom of Proverbs 18:22 (NKJV): "He who finds a wife finds a good thing and obtains favor from the Lord." The rendering in the original Hebrew is actually "finds a good wife," and the only way to identify if she is good is by knowing her through the binoculars of what is good. The finding is not God's responsibility, but men's. God may have allowed circumstances and situations to line up for people to meet, but marriage, maintenance of marriage, and even divorce are the result of man's choice. "Find" indicates that it is your responsibility and that you are looking. You must be able to identify with what is good such as being respectful and having your best interest at heart. So, you see here why the proceeding information was important. It also implies that if you are not looking, you should not involve yourself and someone else with something you are not ready for. It can only lead to pain and resentment. Don't be forced into marriage based on someone's ultimatum or others' decisions for you. It is something you must choose wisely and willingly.

You must be sound in your choosing, otherwise, whom you decide to marry is a product of your ability or a consequence of your inability to understand whom you need. Therefore, maturity is required in the decision. You must visualize what good looks like. At times we are drawn by superficial appearances, but the goal should be not to objectify her and blur the ability to know her thoroughly. Outer appearance will change over time. Building with purpose in mind has a greater value than simply building without intention. A vision is important because it has a future in mind. The aspects we covered as the man plays an important role in how you see yourself. Typically, physically the "Good Wife, helps with the budget and makes sure you go to the Doctor when you should. It is the good wife that brings favor to your life.

Building relationships does not start with marriage. Marriage is the result that stems from a friendship that began before the idea of marriage was presented. It contains learning and relearning. First, you are required to learn how to coexist in one space after operating according to your own rules. Then you have to constantly relearn her, as she changes over time. It is a merger of personalities, views, opinions, and ideas. The blueprint does not call for you to construct her; however, it does require you to reconstruct the way you think so that your capacity is expanded to build together. You have a responsibility to get to know her, just as she has a responsibility to get to know you. The sustainability of your relationship depends on it.

Genesis 2:22 (NKJV) states, "Then the rib which the Lord God had taken from man He made into a woman, and He brought her to the man." Rib in Hebrew is *Tsela*, meaning "side." This could mean a literal rib, but in addition, it could also mean a functional side of him. In this case, it would make sense. She was taken out of him, so with Eve, he is reintroduced to himself. Technically, Eve was another side of Adam. Those two sides make one. The side that is both emotional and reciprocal. To put this into perspective, let us view Adam's wife, Eve, as the other side of him. In addition, let us view our spouse as the other side of us. This leads us to re-evaluate how we see them. You neither abuse nor are selfish against yourself. It is impossible to compete against you. It is self-contradictory. Note that when God created man, he was complete and lacking nothing, which would indicate a side of him was removed.

The woman was pulled out of the man, which means she had already existed in him. Therefore, a man and a woman seem to fit uniformly. The woman is that side of the man that was required to replenish the earth. He is the seed man. The man and his seed are not conducive without the egg and "womb man." As the "womb man," she takes what he provides and immediately attempts to multiply it. In all segments, she is a multiplier, a designed benefit. We see this in reproduction, emotions, speech, and analytics. This is her nature. She is a side of us that we are not quite familiar with, but we must learn this side, so that we may become one. Adam had the privilege of having his wife pulled from him, but as for us, we must find, learn about, and build a relationship with her. The key to oneness is learning the other person and operating as one in each other's own designed function.

Ephesians 5:31-33 (KJV) states, "For this cause shall a man leave his father and mother, and shall be joined unto his wife, and they two shall be one flesh." There is implied that information can be missed if the thought is not deconstructed. When you were a child, your parents supplied your needs, so you must move from being supplied to being a supplier. A man must be positioned to leave his mother and father physically, mentally, emotionally, and financially; however, his preparation will determine how he transitions. For instance, you can be married but still depend on your parents to provide for you in all those categories above. I will expound on this in the explanation of the Husband being the head. Therefore, learning independence before marriage rather than at marriage is critically important. To leave suggests a place of stability or a place in which one can manage the affairs of marriage.

Spiritually, you must believe the same thing, not generally but specifically. God is a generic term. To some, God can be a fish or tree, or many other things to others. Doctrine must be consistent. Ask them about Romans 10:9-10 or Colossians 1:13 and witness them in this light during courtship. Their relationship with Christ will be imminent in their relationship with you. Remember, they are not going to be perfect, but neither will you. People are who they are, so if you are hoping someone will change how they believe during the course of the marriage, then you are setting yourself up for disappointment. Don't unequally yoke yourself to others for selfish reasons, like she is externally beautiful, or sex. Look for substance, like the heart of that person who gives life through her activities and expression.

Ephesians 5:32 (KJV)"Leave his father and mother" was the law of the first mention in Genesis, and it was mentioned again in the four gospels, and then again in the epistles where Paul grants doctrinal explanation. Becoming one flesh is imperative to marital success. Its emphasis implies that this statement is of great importance. When you look at the pretext, it mentions "leave mother and father," so the "be" one flesh" here is more about emerging to where you witness the results. It is to "move out of or away from something and come into view" (Oxford Dictionary). Our belief in the gospel moved us from darkness to light. When reading the pretext, introduces a process of becoming in the instance of both the husband and wife. The change of view or perspective we had from before believing the gospel to after believing is like that which occurs after the man leaves his mother and father. Concerning the man, there is a shift in how he sees things. It is from one-dimensional to include also what she sees. Paul then concludes that his message on husband and wife was centered on the message of Christ and the church.

To further open this narrative, I will explain through the analogy of a teacher using an abstract painting to teach a lesson on perspectives. She asks all students to explain what they see in the painting. Each person would explain from their perspective. There is a possibility that everyone will see it differently. Their views could be related to what they have been exposed to, their influences, and their experiences. It would indicate that their views are different, but not necessarily wrong. It is their truth about the picture. It is necessary to learn from others, to see their truth, and to get a well-rounded perspective. For example, you may offend your wife and not know you have done so, because how you view or process a certain situation may be different. It is important to learn how the other person sees the same thing differently. This better equips you to manage that scenario. To become in marriage is to see the big picture inclusively with her in view. This will help you empathize even if your view looks extremely different.

Amos 3:3 (KJV) states, "Can two walk together, except they be agreed?" The reality of the believer are two people have to be in the same space, valuing each other from the onset, knowing that they are both going in the same direction. You can't place confidence in hoping that one or the other will later change their mind to walk in the same direction. It means you are aligned on some core principles like that above. You will walk in disappointment and resentment, expecting someone to change when they have their own free will. If you change for a person, and not for yourself, you become disappointed, because you are no longer yourself. It takes enormous effort to pretend. No one wins, because your disappointment will become evident in your expression towards her. This scripture seems to suggest being like-minded or having things in common because there is not much deviation in each person's character. We must be content with the knowledge of "what you see is what you get." This means if nothing changes, you are happy with that person.

1 Peter 3:7 (KJV) makes this explicit: "Likewise, ye husbands, dwell with them according to knowledge, giving honour unto the wife, as unto the weaker vessel, and as being heirs together of the grace of life; that your prayers be not hindered." You will have to follow the writer's discourse to build on what he is trying to communicate. He starts with the wife's submission to her husband, then to the husband honoring or placing value on the wife. This presents reciprocity and cause and effect, which indicates your actions can affect the outcome of the relationship. Finally, in v.7 he uses the words "weaker vessel," which seem to suggest that the lack of honoring her may have a greater effect on her. Many conclude that "weaker vessel" meant physical strength, but this may also relate to how she will process how she feels, taking things to heart.

For example, when you are married, how you treat her publicly is as important as how you do in private. There must be a level of consistency. For all general purposes, we sometimes don't consider what position we put the other person in with our actions. For the man, being a protector not only entails the physical but also her mind and emotions. Things that you might consider as insignificant can end up disastrous in the long term. Some public mistakes can damage your spouse's feelings in a way that may be irrevocable. It is the exposure because not only does she sees it, but it has exposure outside of her area of control. With social media advances, you are one click away from information that can't be recanted. Words and actions sometimes leave scars and embarrassment for life.

Deal with her according to knowledge. The word that comes to mind is "idiosyncrasy," which is "a mode of behavior or way of thought peculiar to an individual." From the moment you met her, you began to learn how what you say or do affects her either positively or negatively. You are only as successful as the knowledge you have of the person you are in a relationship with, so becoming a student and learning about her is critically important. Miles Monroe states, "whatever you give a woman she multiplies it, gives it life, and gives it back. If you give her love, she multiplies it, gives it life, and gives it back, but if you give her trouble, she also multiplies it, gives it life, and gives you hell."

Ephesians 5:21-24 (MSG) states, "Out of respect for Christ, be courteously reverent to one another.... The husband provides leadership to his wife the way Christ does to his church, not by domineering but by cherishing. So just as the church submits to Christ as he exercises such leadership, wives should likewise submit to their husbands." Those who lack understanding think manhood in marriage centers around keeping the wife in check by controlling, isolating, or forcing her to do as he says. This result is due to either a lack of intelligence or a man's insecurities. She was never built to be controlled through intimidation but rather designed to be led through demonstrations of love. Remember, we all have a will, and those who are in a relationship are there by choice. A woman who is in Christ willingly submits to a man who demonstrates Christ in his actions towards her but finds a way to rebel in her heart against the man who operates through intimidation. She will find a way to dishonor him. A woman will not follow a man she doesn't trust to lead.

1 Corinthians 7:3 (KJV) states, "Let the husband render unto the wife due benevolence: and likewise, also the wife unto the husband." "Render" means "to give away from oneself." Remember: his role is sacrificial. He is to put her needs before his own, and in the process, she reciprocates his sacrifice, thus completing the writer's statement of "likewise also the wife...." Her action is a reaction to your action or activity. It is the attention that is owed her given to her unfragmented. It has much to do with those things that prevent you from giving away from yourself to her, like obstructions. Obstructions are the roadblock to both giving and receiving. These obstructions can be both internal and external in nature. This means something external can require attention that subtracts from the attention required at home. This could be outside family issues like parents, other outside interests, or job demands. These things can consume one to a point that they can cause a person to neglect the needs required in marriage. Even when unintentional, those unmet needs can lead to frustrations, such as emotional, mental, financial, or even sexual. In this case, an intentional conversation for realigning priorities must be had. Inactivity will comatose the relationship. "If you don't value your relationship, God won't value it for you.

I emphasize this next statement because it is very important. Intimacy is not sex but can lead to it. It takes a mechanism to shift her from one state of being to another, mentally, emotionally, and physically. Women need a mechanism as a gear that turns their body requirements from one place to a place where they can receive the physical act. Men and women are different, and their need for sex is different. Therefore, this means that achieving the experience can also be different. You may be in the mood, but she must get in the mood.

This means that details may require a conversation addressing unresolved issues because she can't process closeness outside of it. Intimacy is a continuous conversation and details to her may be vital. The closure to those things could be simply getting an understanding of the things in question. Remember, details here are a necessity. She may have a dozen things in her head that are obstructions, such as helping kids with homework, washing, figuring out what's for dinner, bills, and issues at work, so sex is the last thing on her mind. Be creative in helping her unpack some of the things carefully because if done in the wrong manner, you can create yet another obstruction. It sounds complicated, but it is not if you deal with her according to knowledge. She needs security, so cuddling and mental stimulation are always a plus. Protect her emotions and be a good steward of the relationship. Just because you are a good provider, doesn't translate to being a good relationship project manager.

Rendering is one but what you render is another. In the earlier text, it mentions rendering "benevolence." It means to present it to her the way she needs to see it. Her affection may look like holding hands or being secure that responsibilities are taken care of in the home. Just like "Respect" may be viewed by you as a way of her rendering affection to you. Let's pay close attention to Proverbs 5:18 (KJV) "Let thy fountain be blessed: and rejoice with the wife of thy youth." This implies a rejuvenated and regenerated relationship. It indicates that as you continue to grow, so shall this revitalize, like the first time, affection towards each other. However, it requires participation that rekindles the original flame. Below is just one of a few.

Compliments, Notes, and Coupons

> Proverbs 25:11 (NAS) *"Like apples of gold in settings of silver Is a word spoken in right circumstances."*

Baby, your smile is equivalent to an enormous sunray.
Your brilliance pierces the clouds of a gloomy day.
Even when the clouds hang over our home,
for they may...
Your persona has the tendency to force them away.
Because You Are Sunshine!

Uplifting, unsuspected simple compliments, words of affirmation, or encouragement, especially written on notes can go a long way. Because I am poetic and I have lived it, I know how simple words can make another smile or laugh could be the difference between a good or bad day. Just as the wrong words at the wrong time can create chaos.

Compliments are important. Notes and coupons are good options. I have a good friend who is notorious for this. He would send the women in his life "free hugs" daily via email just to make their day, and it worked. When compliments are a part of your everyday sentiments, she begins to realize this affection is not made just to get something at the moment. Your intentions are genuine, and the consistency validates your intentions. Remember, it is easy to sit in a barber or beauty shop and compliment people who do not play a significant part in your life, and then neglect the ones whom you live with daily and love the most. For relationship security, she needs to be reminded of her relevance. That you only have eyes for her. When you don't, it raises more questions than you have answers for.

These small memoirs practiced in a relationship have a spontaneous way of stimulating passion with minimal sacrifice. This concept generally has the least number of words and effort, but is most effective, and efficient, and is one the least expensive ways to spark romance in your marriage and make your feeling known. It also frees a spouse to make moves without questioning if the timing is right. Each person creates coupons based on the other desires, wants, and needs. I need to pause right here to qualify this, it is not about your wants but those of your partner. Understanding and fulfilling your spouse's love language is very important. With your partners' desires in mind, you can then create a variety of coupons for hugs, kisses, massages, a night out for dancing, quality time, or intimacy. This gives the other person the opportunity to both redeem and offer services. The women may receive completed chores from their handymen while the men's signature dish is made. I know, in some cases, men are the cooks, and the women are similarly handy. Think of it as "Creativity over Capital." This section is a free spark of passion.

Mix things up making them a little more interesting by handing out a coupon for something you don't normally do. This shows effort on the part of the service provider. On a more serious note, it could be a prayer coupon or even some time alone. Leave a note when departing for work like "I hate to go to work today because that means I will be apart from you," or make bold statements like, "You are a masterful creation--every curve and bend, and when I get home later, I intend to explore the details." Believe it or not, simple little notes like this breathe new excitement and anticipation. Small disagreements and misunderstandings can be a catalyst that divides relationships, and in the same way, small appreciations can be the glue that keeps them together. Vacations and going out on dates are not always an option, but you should at least plan ahead and strive, within reason, to spend quality time together. Be intentional and set aside one day a week to dedicate to each other. With busy schedules, you can easily lose track of each other in the process. It is not always easy when you have kids, but from time to time find a babysitter, so you can spend time with each other. This is a good way to break the monotony but be resourceful when doing so. You are drawn closer through these small gestures and become more passionate. While men or visual, women are engaged by what she hears, so words are useful when used appropriately. Today, we are inspired and become active by applying God's written word to our lives, so it is important to write ideas down. These thoughts are then saved and later serve as a reminder. You can read the note as often as desired and those special moments are relived over again.

We also must be conscious and cautious with our words. We have often heard "Sticks and stones may break my bones, but words will never hurt me" but the reality is, that words do hurt. When someone you care about says harmful words, it can leave a lasting impairment that in some instances can have an everlasting effect. On the unneeded may lead him to search for companionship that allows him to operate in his natural position as a man. This can conclude with - an extramarital affair. It is not always about what you hear, but from whom you hear it. When the right words are spoken and heard with the correct timing, those words can ultimately be the resurrection of your marriage. Never leave anything concerning your feelings about your lover up to question. Kind words of appreciation and support are especially needed in a marriage when couples are facing obstacles. Be mindful of your spouse's needs and reassure them that you are standing by their side with support and encouragement. It all comes down to recognizing what is of value to you. That should be your spouse.

EXCERPT: THE EXTENSION OF MAN

First, I would like to honor all men who have done everything they can to provide for their children. I would like to honor all mothers who have been a foundation for children whose fathers were absent. The pandemic highlighted what has existed for ages: male nonexistence. Absentee fathers who are quick to make babies, but passive when it comes to acknowledging fatherhood and taking responsibility. When I see young women and their kids being evicted after losing their jobs, the same old questions arise. Where are the men? I understand that some men desire to be a part of their children's lives but are not allowed by the mother. Allow the courts to work through this issue but don't give up on your children. As men, we are responsible for building and developing every child we produce, so the conundrum would be if raising your children were a job, could you honestly say you showed up for work every day?

> "Behold, children are a heritage from the Lord, the fruit of the womb a reward." (Psalm 127:3(AMPC).

The use of "lo or behold" in the text is imperative. It implies that what follows it is of vital importance and requires focus and attention. The emphasis here is children are a gift from God. The word heritage means possession. It implies something of value has been placed in your care. It also denotes the receiver of this gift should not take the gift or the responsibilities lightly. Children are the DNA and printed image or merged blueprint of their parents. They are the product of your procreation. Their total identity is encased within this genetic code. Their appearance, physical identity, and even mental capacity. Height, eye color, physical characteristics, but also predisposed health issues. Knowing who they are is important in knowing what they may be predisposed to. When the father is absent, much of this knowledge may go undiscovered. In this, you deny them knowledge of who they are. In the possession of children, they will require guidance. When what is required from the father is missing, the child goes without. Sometimes the mere absence of the father has implications. Guidance is as equally important as understanding their genetics. It is a combination of knowing where you came from and the direction in which they are going, a history of their past, and a roadmap of their future.

They have your DNA what about your presence? It is something about the presence that grants identification. There is a need to see themselves in you. My son has grown into his own man, but when he was a kid, he would step into my shoes when I take them off when getting off from work. He mentioned he wanted to be like me when he grew up. He was very impressionable. He watched me and identified himself with me. I recall him finishing a scripture I was preaching. This is because I was present. Even in this, I wish I could get back the moments I missed. Amazing what a child misses when the father is absent.

In an article, "pediatric associates of Franklin", It states "Fathers not only influence who we are inside but how we have relationships with people as we grow. The way a father treats his child will influence what he or she looks for in other people. Friends, lovers, and spouses will all be chosen based on how the child perceived the meaning of the relationship with his or her father. The patterns a father sets in the relationships with his children will dictate how his children relate with other people." The impact of a father is great, but what happens if he is not present? We will show the impact later.

> *Then he blessed Joseph and said, "May the God before whom my grandfather Abraham and my father, Isaac, walked—the God who has been my shepherd all my life, to this very day,16 the angel who has redeemed me from all harm— may he bless these boys. May they preserve my name and the names of Abraham and Isaac. And may their descendants multiply greatly throughout the earth" (Genesis 48:15-16 NLT).*

In the text, the grandfather, Israel, speaks a blessing to Joseph's sons. Joseph refused it initially because he was concerned about the firstborn getting the blessing. In that eastern culture, the custom was that the firstborn would get the birthright. The truth is, that God wants all children to be blessed, so Jacob had to explain to Joseph why he was blessing both sons. The takeaway for us today is that a child believes what a parent believes about them, and that is their mantle for success. A father must speak a blessing upon his children. It is quite the journey when trying to mold a young child into adulthood. They need to be encouraged and told that they are great and convinced that success is theirs if they believe and work toward it. Adversely, when you criticize your children, they don't stop loving you, they stop loving themselves~ Abel Damina.

Usually, children will attempt to make their parents proud because they require their approval. In addition, they look to their father for security. If the father is absent, then an uncle, Grandfather, coach, or another male can teach them what a father is supposed to look like. Every parent varies in their perspectives on rearing kids, and they become the premise from where that teaching begins. Your child must know that they have just as much a right to success as others, thereby teaching them to be comfortable being themselves and to have the desire and confidence to conquer whatever challenge that may exist.

Train your children

> "Train up a child in the way he should go:
> and when he is old, he will not depart from
> it" (Proverbs 22:6 KJV).

Train your child up because they will have to combat the influence of the untrained and the self-trained. They are facing an age of information warfare. Philosophies and opinions flood social media and if they are not strong-minded, they can easily be drawn into deception like that that was introduced by the serpent in the garden. They may be presented with an alternative view of God's Word. Construction starts with you being prepared to take on the responsibility because if you're not, it will be projected, and they will witness your insecurities. The frustration could lie in not knowing how to relate and this will cause you to be ineffective as a teacher. They are great imitators, so early on they learn based on your actions. It is necessary that you fulfill your obligation because your legacy depends on your actions.

When you are building something, you need to make sure you have the right tools or find someone who does and can also help you build. Sometimes, we speak in mysteries to our kids relating to the environment they grew up in, to which they have no conceptual understanding. We live in an era in which our kids need more than "Back in my day," when I was a kid, Because I told you so," and "I'll give you something to cry about." They need to be polished to live in the day for which they exist. Back in the day, we had one home phone that everyone had to share. We had to read to get information, and information about what was happening was not instant. It is the total opposite for them. Discipline and communication are still necessary. Your responsibility as a parent has not changed. Just like a man learning about his wife, he must learn what his children are exposed to. Only then can you guide them through it. Technology, outdated slang words, and phrases our generation used are now obsolete. Again, you don't have to be a Superman, just be super wise. Relate to them based on how they understand, to make a valid point. This simply means using their interest as a teaching tool. To be a good teacher, you must also be a good listener.

We build from the framework based on our exposures and we sometimes are convinced that we have done a good job rearing our kids based on this. If we are honest, we gave what we felt they needed from our perspective, without understanding that their time may be presenting them with a new set of challenges. This would allow us to expand our approach to rearing differently. Many of our youth and teenage years look quite different than those of today. We didn't have cell phones with access to any and every App available to mankind. There were no cyber-bullies or Facebook that controlled emotions based on likes. Teach them to love themselves, so they are not seeking superficial things.

As referenced previously, we build based on how we were built. Build with foresight, so that they can rise above their insecurities. To everything you build, there must also exist the desire to maintain. In this, you have an opportunity to rebuild the area where they have experienced brokenness. Doing this early can teach them how to recover, rather than embracing it through internalization. One of the most thought-provoking quotes I have ever read was by Frederick Douglass. He suggested, "It is easier to build strong children than to repair broken men." It is important to give direction, correction, and attention so that the culmination of your actions paints the big picture. That picture is that they may become motivated for success. Give them a chance to fall and allow them to try to get back up and in the process teach to how.

There are many things we avoid talking about because

we are concerned about "when is the right time." With the age of technology so advanced now, it may already be too late. We must think beyond how we grew up and relate to the present to bridge the generation gap. They have access to the information we did not have at the same age, so we can't use our past timetable to determine how to talk to them now. We should start teaching our children at a much younger age than when we received it. They have access to cell phones, computers, and Google commands, so the information is available and on-demand just from their voice request. This means, that if you are not providing information, they can still obtain it. Would you rather share it, so you know the content, or would you prefer they receive information that does not coincide with your beliefs?

They are exposed to disinformation warfare that they have not been prepared to fight. We faced challenges in our generation, but they face our challenges on steroids. They face sex trafficking, diseases that kill, and terrorism in schools and communities. Their awareness must be heightened and their discernment keen. They have the task of adults, such as being able to evaluate if someone walks into their school and if they are a threat or not. They must be spiritual, intelligent, and streetwise to prevent deception. Their understanding of money management, investments, socialization, education, sex, etc., is vital, but having God in their lives is not optional, but mandatory.

I grew up in the church; both of my grandfathers were pastors. They also worked in some facet or another. At some point, my dad purchased an Animated Bible for kids, so that we could become acquainted with the bible at home on Wednesdays. He also woke us up on Saturdays to go to work with him at his shop. Today, I see value in both of those separate spectrums. I am rooted in the faith which has always been a part of my life, and I have learned work ethics and a trade that is at my disposal when I need it. When it states in Proverbs 22:6 that a child is trained "in the way he should go," this could also imply that you should steer them in the right direction and teach them to utilize the tools at their disposal. They need to be both spiritually fit and earthly fit. They are ready for heaven and able to have an influence on the earth with their jobs, skills, and talents so that the ministry is wherever they are.

Ephesians 6:4(NKJV) and you, fathers, do not provoke your children to wrath but bring them up in the training and admonition of the Lord. You would have to read all of Ephesians to understand the writer's message. It is about relationships and how they work in conjunction with each other. This passage should jump from the page because it is specifically addressed to fathers. The relationship that you develop will be the relationship you inherit. The way you nurture that relationship and the effort you give will determine the outcome. "Indifference and neglect often do much more damage than outright dislike," says -J.K. Rowling. There are at least three things that can provoke a child to wrath. These are abandonment, abuse, and pride. Wrath defined by The NAS Greek Lexicon is movement or agitation of the soul, impulse, desire, any violent emotion, but especially anger." "Parents who leave their children, with or without good reason, can cause psychological damage to the child."

Can you imagine what a child goes through when they

feel unwanted? Yet, there is an estimated 40,000 infants that enter foster care yearly due to neglect or abuse according to Huffington Post. The sad truth about us as men is due to momentary pleasure with women, with whom we never intended to have long-term relationships. You were selfish and just wanted sex, and the results are unwanted children. Some kids never get to know their parents, and then there are those whose fathers live three blocks down the street and have no desire to take on their responsibility. He boastfully denies his claim to his child. I want to expose the big picture to present the burden men have placed on society and the brokenness they have placed on children, who grow up to be broken adults. Could you imagine your kid, created from your DNA, sitting in the crowd where all their friends' dad is sitting in the audience at their event, and they are angry and broken that you are nowhere to be found? What if you were that child?

Can you envision the bitterness that they feel toward you because you don't even have the decency to be a man? It is perplexing, that a man would not want to build a relationship with his child by at least spending time with them on the weekend or giving them a gift on birthdays or holidays. When this happens, the little girl ends up with daddy issues. This is when she goes out and finds a man who treats her like a girl, simply because she never had a father. The boys have identity issues because he does not know what a man looks like. They are embedded with emotions to which they have no answer because the one who holds the key is avoiding them. You have just created scars that someone has the burden of carrying. You provoke them to anger not only toward you but life itself.

The Impact of Change

It was February 2014 when I told my son I had gotten another job, his first response was, "Does this mean you will be off on weekends?" You see, the year before I was working at an unstable job. As a ripple effect, this made our time together inconsistent which made it challenging for me to spend quality time with my son. It was critical because the weekends were supposed to be our time. It was that statement, at that moment, when I realized that spending time together was just as important to him as it was to me in that season. There were moments he required it and it was missed. These moments were missed, and we could never get them back. Getting a new job, was the platform for him to express how he felt, and what spending time truly meant.

I wonder how many children want to spend time with their fathers, but they can only wonder about brokenness. It is in those moments impressions in their young minds are produced, and they think about themselves as abandoned. Based on impressions that do not appear, they will forever be in search of their identity. I challenge all men who have lost valuable contact in the past to go back and rebuild those relationships. Be instrumental in the developmental stage.

When a parent is sitting down and taking the time to help the child with homework, talking to or practicing a sport with a child, it starts and solidifies the bonding process. This is extremely important. When I was young, we would sit at the dinner table as a family, and we would talk. This was the pre-cell phone, one TV, and one house phone era. We were almost forced to communicate out of pure boredom. When everyone was comfortable with communication there was nothing hidden.

Children should be able to approach their parents with anything on their minds, and this is very critical in developing solid relationships. Like any other relationship, if you close that door, they will be least likely to feel comfortable opening up to you again. With the changing of the times, everyone has become too busy to spend time together. We don't even sit around the dinner table anymore. The father watches Sports Center in the living room all the time, the mom is watching her favorite reality TV show in the bedroom, while the kid is in their room doing whatever. The enemy is launching a subtle attack on the house. The enemy is dividing the house, and no one is even aware of it.

The greatest lesson that can be learned is to acknowledge a mistake without shifting blame around. When a child is aware of his actions and matures enough to make good decisions, he then becomes accountable and enters a season of manhood transformation. Studies show that when parents are involved in a child's education, the child has a higher success rate. Training a child is not an option, but a mandate from the Word of God. Is it not funny how some kids grow up and want to be just like their parents? This means that developing a healthy relationship with them could have a powerful influence on their life.

Situations of Change

I was just thinking of the parable of the protocol son from an observation of love, patience, and forgiveness, a complete portrait of grace. Ultimately, this parable is about God's forgiveness but also portrays life circumstances and their impact on relationships. The father demonstrates love, patience, and forgiveness, while the brother does not. It is two people responding differently to the same situation, but each clearly from an angle from which they see it. The welcoming back is a demonstration of what God does for us. In some cases, we and our children may see things differently. In the case of children, you may have to look at their point of view with grace, simply because it is a perspective with which they have no experience in dealing with. When a new child, new wife (stepmom), or even you, as a new father is added to the equation, it can be foreign to them.

It is not that they do not want to respond, they simply don't know how without instruction. They, like us, at times may not know how to feel or act when this occurs. Although we hope our children will think like us, it is a new experience for them, and they sometimes need guidance through the process. Often time they become disconnected because someone seems to take the space they once occupied. They then start to question where they fit into this new experience. It is in these situations that their ability to adapt to change will determine their success; otherwise, they can easily become displaced. In their search, they are susceptible to finding a fit in rebellion as a cry for attention. What is most difficult, they can be entangled in lifestyles that can take a lifetime to recover from.

Abandonment can be perceived in the context above, but also when a father is absent or unknown. The effect of abandonment is to make children spend a great portion of their lives trying to process why they were not wanted. In addition, they try to find their identity, while acting out how they feel. Abandonment could also mean you are physically present, but mentally and emotionally absent. I encourage men to reach out and give attention to those children whose fathers are not actively present.

The following details the consequences of paternal abandonment, according to statistics:

Safety, mental health, and wellbeing:

- 63% of youth suicides are from fatherless homes (US Dept. Of Health/Census)—5 times the average.
- 90% of all homeless and runaway children are from fatherless homes—32 times the average.
- 85% of all children who show behavioral disorders come from fatherless homes—20 times the average (Center for Disease Control).
- 80% of rapists with anger problems come from fatherless homes—14 times the average. (*Justice and Behavior*, Vol 14, p. 403-26).
- 71% of all high school dropouts come from fatherless homes—9 times the average (National Principals Association Report).

Education:

Fatherless children are twice as likely to drop out of school.

- Children with fathers who are involved in their lives are 40% less likely to repeat a grade in school.
- Children with fathers who are involved in their lives are 70% less likely to drop out of school.
- Children with fathers who are involved in their lives are more likely to get A's in school.
- Children with fathers who are involved in their lives are more likely to enjoy school and engage in extracurricular activities.
- 75% of all adolescent patients in chemical abuse centers come from fatherless homes—10 times the average. (Retrieved from https://the fatherlessgeneration.WordPress.com/statistics, 2010)."

Don't wait for a lifetime to build or even rebuild. Start building now in the place where you are, because there will come a time when your capacity to build will end. Build light in dark places.

Printed in the United States
by Baker & Taylor Publisher Services